THE
KIDS-ONLY CLUB
BOOK

Other Books by Shari Lewis

Magic for Non-Magicians, with Abraham B. Hurwitz

The Tell It-Make It Book

Folding Paper Puppets, with Lillian Oppenheimer

Folding Paper Toys, with Lillian Oppenheimer

Folding Paper Masks, with Lillian Oppenheimer

Making Easy Puppets

Fun with the Kids

Dear Shari

Be Nimble, Be Quick, with Jacquelyn Reinach

Knowing and Naming, with Jacquelyn Reinach

Thinking and Imagining, with Jacquelyn Reinach

Looking and Listening, with Jacquelyn Reinach

THE
KIDS-ONLY CLUB
BOOK

BY SHARI LEWIS

Published by J. P. Tarcher, Inc., Los Angeles
Distributed by Hawthorn Books, Inc., New York

Dedication:
To my mother and father who felt that every
child had something special to offer — even
before that was fashionable.

Acknowledgments:
The author wishes to thank Francis J. Orlaski
of the San Gabriel Boy Scouts of America and
Mina Post of the Angeles Council of the Girl
Scouts of America for their many valuable
suggestions; the California Department of Fish
and Game, for their ideas which were
incorporated into the Conservation Gang
chapter; and especially Ross Olney, for his
considerable help in bringing this diverse
material together.

Library of Congress Catalog Card Number: 76-10507

ISBN: 0-87477-054-8

Jacket and text design and illustrations by The Committee

Manufactured in the United States of America

Published by J. P. Tarcher, Inc.
9110 Sunset Blvd., Los Angeles, Calif. 90069

Published simultaneously in Canada by
Prentice-Hall of Canada, Ltd.
1870 Birchmount Rd., Scarborough, Ontario

1   2   3   4   5   6   7   8   9   0

Contents

Chapter 1
Kids-Only Means "Do-It-Yourself"

A Kids-Only Club is great fun, mainly because *you* are in charge. A Kids-Only Club doesn't have adults around who tell members how everything should be done. The members themselves decide what the club is going to do.

This book will show you how to put together your own Kids-Only Club and how to run meetings and activities.

Now a club is more than a meeting with lots of talk, followed by cookies and milk. That's a party. That isn't a club.

A club brings together, on a regular basis, friends or people who have the same ideas and interests. It brings them together to do something. The "something" that you and your friends decide you want to do is what your club is all about.

The reason for your club may be just to have friends meet together to do fun things and do them on their own. Some of the members might be stamp collectors or sports lovers; others might have magic, square dancing, or model-building as a hobby. In other words, your club could be made up of kids with lots of *different* interests. But when everybody enjoys doing them together as a group, that's reason enough to have a Kids-Only Club.

Or maybe everybody in your group has the *same* interest. It could be raising tropical fish, or planting backyard vegetable gardens, playing rock music or taking long bicycle trips. The nice thing is that with a good club as a base, you can do what you like to do best even better than you can do it by yourself.

Some of the things in this book are easier to do if your club has eight or ten kids in it and will be hard if there are only three or four of you. For in-

Doing Things Together

stance, putting on a play that has eight people in it won't be easy to do if there are only four of you in your club. But you can always reduce the activities to fit the size of your membership. Or, better yet, for big projects like a carnival or craft fair, ask your brothers and sisters to give you a hand just for that special occasion, even if they aren't club members.

All of the activities, games, crafts, and projects in this book can be carried out without having an adult lead the way. There may come a time or two when you might want to ask for some help from a grown-up—after all, adults help each other, too—but you'll find that just following the ideas and suggestions in this book will probably give you all the help you need.

Chapter 2
Lots to Do!

Whether your club is made up of kids who all like to do the same things or who want to do a bunch of different things, there's lots to do.

Some of the things you'll do just for the fun of it. Some of the activities in this book are not only enjoyable, but will help your club make money.

This book will tell you how to put on craft fairs and carnivals. It will tell you how to make dozens of different crafts, games, and toys, and all sorts of gifts to give and goodies to keep.

It will show you how your club can put on shows with people or puppets, or performances where the group makes magic together.

And since "fun" is anything that makes you feel good, it will also give you ideas about how you can do something to help others: the people in your neighborhood, the animals in the neighborhood, and your neighborhood itself.

You'll discover how to help people by making and collecting toys for children in hospitals and orphanages, by putting on shows for nursery schools or old people's homes, and by helping during charity drives, like TV telethons.

You'll find ways to really help animals by building them homes, feeding them during the winter, and making your neighborhood a better place for them to live. And while you are making it better for the animals, you'll find how to make it better for the whole neighborhood; you can adopt a plot, begin a clean-up campaign, or have a bike-athon for your favorite project.

You won't know all the exciting things waiting for you until you get started. And the way to start is this: Decide on one thing you want to do—something you can't do all by yourself—and get together with friends who will do it with you in your very own Kids-Only Club.

Chapter 3
Old Friends, New Friends

Before you start your own club, make sure there is no other club just like it around the block. If there is another club around that does what you want to do, think about joining *it* rather than starting your own. Competition for members could make it hard to get your brand new club off the ground.

Of course, even if there is another club going, you may have a reason why you would rather put together your own. If so, go ahead.

Invite Others

WHO TO INVITE

Okay! You've decided to form your own club.

The first step is to invite everybody to a meeting you think might be interested in joining. You'll probably invite your best friends to the first gathering. If your friends have pals, they can join later.

Most clubs have some rules describing who can join (say, kids on certain blocks, girls in the fifth and sixth grades, kids who like bicycle riding, and so on). Since you are starting this club, you probably have the best ideas about who should belong and who should not. But the best clubs are the ones that welcome any kids who fit the description, not just the ones you might have in mind at the very beginning.

If your club is going to last, let *all* of the members decide which kids are to be invited. That's how long-lasting, strong clubs work.

The More, the Merrier

What you want are active working members. Lots of them. The first people who join are called *charter members*. They can spread the word around that your club is starting.

Local newspapers are a good place to announce a new group and tell what it plans to do.

(In the chapter, "Letting the World Know!" you can read about how to get some newspaper publicity for your club.)

But once you get started, keep your eye out for new members, because after any club gets going, there are always one or two who drop out. Perhaps they are hurt that they were not chosen president or that their suggestions were not acted on by the group. Maybe they had second thoughts about the whole thing or found out that they just didn't have the time for many of the club's activities. Whatever the reason, don't let such dropouts turn off the rest of the group. Quick! If you look, you will find others who will be eager to join.

Chapter 4
What Shall We Do First?

Your folks will probably let you hold the first few meetings in the living room or playroom at home. At this first meeting you'll want to talk about how to put your club together—and how to make it last.

One of the reasons why many adult clubs last and most Kids-Only Clubs do not is that grown-ups have learned that *somebody* must take charge. Every group needs a leader. You want your club to be a Kids-Only Club. No adults. So, first thing, vote on who's to be in charge.

Pick a "temporary chairperson." Even at this first get-together, you'll need somebody to lead and keep things in order.

You'll also need a "temporary secretary" to write things down: suggestions, opinions, and votes. If there is a disagreement later about what was said during the meeting, you can just check this record.

The Ground Rules

When people play an organized game, like baseball or football, they follow ground rules. Everybody agrees ahead of time what the rules are to be and promises to follow them. This is the best way to avoid arguments and to keep the game going. This is the best way to organize a club, too, or any other activity where lots of people are going to be doing things together over a period of time.

You're starting a Kids-Only Club, so do it right, right from the start. At the first meeting make up a list of simple ground rules for your club.

Mention the main *reason* or *purpose* for your club (to put on shows, to run a carnival, to collect and trade stamps, to help animals, or whatever).

The rules should tell about the *members* (who they can be). It should tell all about the *officers* (how many the club will have: president or chairperson, secretary, etc., what these officers' jobs will be, how they are to be elected, how often you will vote for new officers, and so on).

Tell when the club's *meetings* will be held (once a week or once a month, on which days, what time).

Another ground rule to be decided is how many members must be present to take a *vote* on any matter to make it stick.

Don't vote on these suggested ground rules during the first meeting. This list is just for everybody to think about. When members come back for the second meeting, then vote on them, and you will have your club's ground rules. These ground rules are not forever. If members want to change them later, they can be changed like any other law.

These rules are like the Constitution of the United States, and you can call them your club's Constitution.

The Name Game

Another thing you can talk about during the first meeting and vote on during the second is the name for your group. Then the club name can be included in the Constitution too.

The name of some clubs clearly tells the world who they are and what they do (like the Boy Scouts). Some clubs have poetic names (like the Bluebirds). Some have been shortened into a secret word or phrase (like the 4-H Club which stands for Head, Heart, Hands, and Health—now it's not a secret anymore!).

If your club is being formed to get together regularly for sports, it could be called the *B*asketball *A*nd *T*rack *S*portsmen. Then your secret name might be "The BATS." Or if you have a party and carnival group, you could call yourselves "The PACK"—*P*arty *A*nd *C*arnival *K*ids.

At the second meeting with your temporary chairperson in charge, let everyone discuss the names suggested and then vote for one.

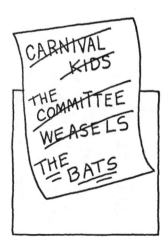

Who's in Charge Here?

Your Vote, Your Secret

Initiation Fee and Dues

Once you have your name and your ground rules, the temporary chairperson and secretary have done their jobs. Now regular officers can be elected. These officers can serve for a month or a year or whatever your club decided in the ground rules. Most clubs have a president, a vice president, a secretary, and a treasurer. The president runs the club, the vice president is in charge when the president is absent, the secretary takes notes and answers letters, the treasurer takes care of money.

You might choose a special name for your officers, depending on the type of club you have. A magic club might have a "Wizard" instead of a president; a club to put on plays and shows might have a "Director," and if you have a club like "The BATS," the person in charge might be called the "Manager."

When you vote for club officers, you don't want to hurt anyone's feelings. So keep your votes secret by having members write their choices on pieces of paper rather than by holding up their hands while everybody watches.

Many of the things that your club will do won't cost any money. Others may cost a little to get started, though they may turn out to be money-making in the end. (For example, to put on a craft fair you'll need to buy supplies, but by the time the craft fair is over, you'll probably have made more money than you spent.)

Start off by deciding on a specific amount (perhaps a dollar) which all members must pay to join. This is an *initiation fee* and will give you something to start with. Then set *dues,* the small amount of money each member will give at each meeting.

The amount of dues can be decided by your group. Don't make your dues high or some members might have to drop out because they can't afford it.

14

The amount of the initiation fee and the dues should also be put in your ground rules.

Now you really have a club, not just a bunch of friends getting together. Your ground rules tell:

1. Name and purpose of your club
2. How to become a member
3. A list of officers, how they are elected, what their jobs are, how long they keep those jobs
4. When the meetings are held
5. Dues and the amount of money a person has to pay to get into the club
6. How many members must vote to make a decision

You will find that it's fun to get organized. Once you set it up right, your club will have a good chance of staying around for a long time.

Here's how most people run their club meetings so that everything can be talked about and decisions made without members getting into arguments:

1. The president calls the meeting to order. (In other words, he gets everybody quiet.)
2. The secretary calls the roll. (Members answer "Here" when their names are called.)
3. The secretary reads the notes made at the last meeting. These notes (called "Minutes") tell what was decided at that last meeting.

Your "Getting Started" Check List

The Meeting Will Come To Order Please

4. The treasurer tells how much money the club has and how it is being spent.

5. Dues are collected.

6. Old business (any matters discussed by the members at the last meeting but not decided on by a vote) is taken care of.

7. Plans for things you want to do in the future are talked about and voted upon. This is called "new business." Sometimes a vote is not taken, so this "new business" becomes "old business" at the next meeting.

8. Then you do whatever you decided to do this time (make your puppets or posters, write the play or news release, construct the games for your carnival, make the decorations for your party, or whatever).

9. At the end of every meeting make absolutely sure that all the members know when and where the next meeting is to be and that you have fully planned what you are going to do at that next get-together. If any member needs to bring something to that meeting, he or she should write a little note about it. Otherwise, when everyone shows up you may not have what you need for your activities.

10. Straighten up. Pick up. Clean up. If you leave your meeting room even neater than you found it, you and your friends will always be welcome back.

You can see that if you follow this list, meetings will run smoothly and fights will be few. Not only that, but you'll get lots of things done, and there will be more fun ahead for all of you.

Chapter 5
A Place of Your Own

A club member's home will work very well as a meeting place the first few times you get together.

The very best Kids-Only Club meeting place will have:

1. Privacy
2. Enough room for all the members
3. A place you can fix up to suit your own activity (this may be hard to find and may be something you have to do without).

If you can't find these things at a club member's home, try a local church or a community center. All these places have meeting rooms. If you have ground rules for running the club, regular officers, and are well organized, you stand a good chance of getting a fine place to meet. A group like yours makes the person or organization that owns the meeting room look good in the community. And as long as you take care of it, you will be welcome.

Renting a meeting room is not the best idea for a new club. Stick with places that come free. So try storekeepers and merchants who might have an interest in the purpose of your group. A coin club could check out the local coin dealers; a model-building club, the local hobby shop; a magic club, the nearest magic store. A back room in a store is a fine meeting place (and sometimes the storekeeper may give you a little financial help too).

Perhaps the parents of a club member have space at their place of business. Other leads for you to follow are schools (call the principal's office and ask if you can meet after hours in the lunchroom, classroom, auditorium, etc.), the YMCA, YWCA, parks and playgrounds (most have buildings for people to get together), libraries (they're very willing to help people in the neighborhood), local police and fire department (they are often happy to develop friendships with young people this way), service clubs (Elks, Eagles, Lions, American Legion, Hadassah, etc.).

Just call up and tell them exactly what you want, and they will put you in touch with a person who can help you.

Chapter 6
Share a Secret, Share a Sign

Lots of organizations have special handshakes and passwords so that members can secretly signal one another or show their friendship without anyone else knowing who isn't in on the secret. Your Kids-Only Club members might like to have just such a password or handshake.

There are other signs too. Your friends could proudly wear a club emblem on their T-shirts or jackets, and a Kids-Only Club Certificate might be given to every member as he or she joins the club to put on the wall of his or her room. These are all great to make and even greater to own.

Your Secret Password and Handshake

The password could be anything at all but probably should have something to do with the purpose of the club. For instance, if your hobby is fish, your password might be "Jaws!" If your hobby is stamp collecting, you could whisper, "Special Delivery!" You can combine the password with a secret sound or whistle for entry to the club meeting.

Of course, there will be many activities where you'll want everyone to know that you're a member of a special club. For these occasions you might design a sign for your club and make it your "official emblem. Members could try their hand at designing it. Once you have voted which one will be your emblem, hang it up on your clubroom wall for all to see. It's not expensive either to have a rubber stamp made of your club emblem to use on any official Kids-Only Club papers, notices, posters.

And if you would like to put your club emblem on a T-shirt, here's how: You will need wax crayons, a T-shirt (one that has been laundered at least once), a clothes iron, and an adult to stand by.

It's a good idea to practice all over an old T-shirt first. This way you can get the technique down perfectly, and when you try it on a newer shirt it will turn out really well.

Slip a shirt cardboard or small bread board into the shirt to stretch the fabric a bit.

Draw your design (in pencil) on the shirt. The emblem design should be high on the chest. To find the right spot, look in the mirror and hold the design in place. Now color in the emblem on the T-shirt, pressing hard on your wax crayons.

Put a piece of waxed paper (waxed side up) under the shirt fabric on which you have crayoned. Place another piece of waxed paper (waxed side down) over your design. Ask the adult who is standing by to set the iron temperature selector for the kind of material you are using. Iron—very slowly—over the top sheet of waxed paper. The heat of the iron will melt the crayon, and the crayon colors will sink right into the threads of the T-shirt.

Remove the waxed paper and you're done.

Once your crayon colors have been ironed in, your T-shirt can be washed again and again in cold or lukewarm water, and the colors will not run or fade. But don't put your club T-shirt in with other laundry. Handwash it only.

You can use this same method to make banners to hang on the wall, place mats to give as presents, or club tablecloths to use at parties. Wouldn't it be fun to have every member of the club sign his or her name in crayon on a Kids-Only Club tablecloth? You can keep adding autographs as your club grows.

When you have enough money in your treasury, you can even send a copy of your emblem to a "patch" maker and have a jacket patch made for each member. This makes a super gift for new members. You'll find patch makers in your city listed under "Emblems" in the Yellow Pages of the telephone book.

Each member will enjoy making and having an official Kids-Only Club Certificate to hang on his or her wall.

This might be made out of a decorated paper plate and could include the club emblem, the name of the club, the date on which it was started, the name of the member, the date on which he or she became a member of the club, their membership number, and anything else you think is important.

This certificate could also have a space for the member to write down the different offices that he or she holds over a period of time and the various committees on which he or she has served. The club certificate can be signed by the person who is the leader or president of the club at the time the member joined.

The plate can be decorated in many ways. You might want to cover the outer rim of the plate with glue and stick on tiny pebbles or twigs (cut in ½-inch lengths, placed so they cross on top of one another), rice, dried coffee grounds, shells, noodles or macaroni (soaked in poster paint and then dried), or even tiny bits of papers of various colors.

Now cut a piece of paper in the shape of the inner circle of the plate and write the information you want in crayon or felt-tipped pen. Then glue it into the middle of the decorated plate. If you attach a looped string to the back with glue or tape, you can then hang the club certificate on your bedroom wall.

With your ground rules, your officers, meeting plans, and emblems, you're on your way to being the most organized and successful club in your neighborhood.

Chapter 7
Get Ready, Get Set

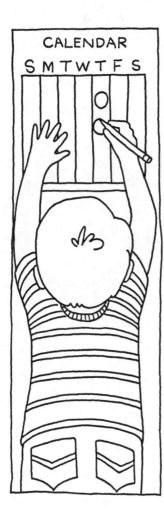

There are many things your club can do, but at the beginning it's best to do them one at a time. Later, when your club has been going on for a while you can plan a carnival, put on a puppet show, and even run a conservation gang project—all at the same time if you wish.

Start by letting everyone pick one activity that he or she would like to do most. Talk about each idea, and then take a vote. Most of the members of the club should agree on the project before you start.

Some activities can be enjoyed with little planning at the very next meeting (like making puppets or playing some games). Others (like putting on a play) will take a number of meetings to prepare.

This chapter is going to give general ideas on how to run any event where you invite other people. Other chapters tell you exactly what to do. For a backyard carnival, see "Running a Carnival." Craft fairs and the things to make, do, and sell, are described in the chapter on "Craft-Making and Giving Craft Fairs." If you're planning a play, see "Staging a Play." If puppets are your pleasure, turn to "Doing a Puppet Show." And to know how to put on a magic show, turn to the chapter on "Making Magic."

Pick the Day

The day you pick for your event should be the day that is best for most of your members. Look at a calendar and discuss the date you want to choose because it would be a shame to pick a day for your play or carnival and then find out that half the members have piano lessons or dental appointments or are going out of town with their parents. It's not always easy to find one day that's perfect for every-

body, but if you plan ahead your Kids-Only Club event day will be the day people set aside and save so they can be there.

Give your Kids-Only Clubbers plenty of time before that date to work up to the project you have chosen. Preparing for that party or carnival or craft fair can be almost as much fun as giving it, so don't cheat yourself by rushing into it.

Think about all the different things you have to do—actually write out a list and figure out how much time each one will take. Two weeks isn't enough time for a craft fair but would be perfect for a picnic in the backyard or a nearby park.

One general rule to remember: Everything takes just a little longer than you think it will, so keep that in mind when you set the day. Remember, if you don't remember, you'll forget.

If you are counting on the public coming, be sure to advertise early enough to let everybody know that you're having a special event and all are invited. You'll find some good ideas on how to do that in the chapter on "Letting the World Know!"

Good Timing

Think about the audience you want to attract, and choose a time and day when they would be free to come.

Kids can seldom make it during mealtimes. Adults don't like to get up too early on weekends. Important ball games on TV will cut into your crowd, and so will the big rummage sale at the church two blocks away if it is being held on the same day.

Picking and Following the Leader

Now that you have picked an event and the date, have your members decide who will be in charge. This might be the person who had the idea for the event in the first place, or it could be any other working member of the club. One thing is certain: Somebody has to be in charge to make sure that everything is in place when it's needed on that day and that everyone is doing the job he or she said would be done.

Divide and Conquer

A club has the power to do many things, because you can get many different people doing different jobs all at the same time. Rather than all the members doing every job and being in on every decision, divide the kids into groups of those who can do one thing best.

For example, a couple of your members may be good at crafts and enjoy making posters or costumes. Others who are good talkers may be able to get local storekeepers to put those posters in their windows.

One kid can't be good at everything, so make the most of all the different talents and interests your members have by forming smaller groups. These are called committees. They are made up of kids who have a certain skill, as well as those who just want to be part of the project.

The leader will ask one person to head up a committee for each of the jobs that needs to be done. That "Head of the Committee" can ask for volunteers or choose other members to help.

For example, if you were going to run a carnival some of your committees might be:

1. The Location and Booth Committee. This group would be in charge of finding a good place for the carnival to be held. They plan where the booths will go and get them ready on the day of the event.

2. The Games Committee. This committee would be in charge of choosing, making, and testing the games to be played at the carnival.

3. The Prize Committee. If the carnival is going to award prizes to the winners at each booth, this group will collect those prizes and give them out to the lucky ones on the big day.

4. The Publicity Committee. These kids are responsible for getting people to come to your carnival.

5. The Carnival Day Committee. This group is in charge of running the booths during the carnival.

These are only examples. Your Kids-Only Club should decide for itself what committees are needed and what their jobs will be.

Each committee should have someone who reports to the person in charge of the event. This person keeps track of what is happening, what has been done, and what still needs to be done. If something isn't getting done right, the person in charge asks other people to pitch in so the job is finished in plenty of time.

And now that you know how to run a carnival, let's go to one.

Chapter 8
Running a Carnival

Real, live carnivals are almost a thing of the past, but your Kids-Only Club can bring them back —right into your own backyard. All you need are booths, games, prizes, barkers, people to run the games—and you're in business. If you don't have a backyard, try a park, the schoolyard, or other open, flat spaces around town, but first get permission from the school, the park supervisor, or the owner to use these places.

To put on a successful carnival, there are a number of things your club should do ahead of time.

1. Somebody should be put in charge.
2. Games must be chosen and tested.
3. Prizes should be arranged.
4. Booths need to be built and decorated.
5. The carnival should be advertised.
6. Club members to run the booths need to be chosen.

Let's take these one by one.

The Head Barker

Every project needs someone who is in charge. Since carnivals have barkers, let's call the boss the Head Barker. The club can elect a Head Barker or the president can appoint somebody.

The Head Barker keeps track of everything that needs to be done and makes sure that the people who have taken on the above jobs are doing them. If they need help, the Head Barker finds other club members who will lend a hand. Two hands, if necessary.

How Much To Charge

The Head Barker can suggest how much to charge for each game, and the whole club can then vote on these suggestions. Different games

should have different prices, depending on how many points can be won. Keep everything inexpensive. Five or ten cents a game should be about right, and some games should be played just for fun—no price, no points, and no prize.

For any event open to the public—especially for one where they will be spending money—you'll want to be sure that everything works pretty much as you planned. Athletes practice their sports, actors rehearse lines, and you, too, should try out all the parts of your carnival. This means that you need to test the games to make sure that most of your club members really enjoy playing them. If they

Testing and Selecting the Games

Point Tickets

Prizes

enjoy them, so will everybody else. Everybody doesn't have to like every game, but a majority of the club members should give their approval. Each person should also be given the chance to suggest his or her own favorite game and have it tested by the members.

Along with testing the games to see how they work best (how many tosses a player should be allowed, how far from the target he or she should stand, etc.), you should test all the parts of the carnival. You can do this by putting on a carnival for yourselves and maybe a few outside friends to make sure that everything is in working order. With this "rehearsal," you'll be able to decide how well your customers will have to do to be winners at each game, how many points to give them for winning, and even how many points they will need to win in order to earn the prize.

A good way to award prizes is to give "points" to each person who wins at one of the carnival games. The point tickets which are given to the winners should be made up in advance. Points are like money at the carnival. You use them to "buy" prizes, so make them look like no other "money" you've ever seen before. Take a sheet of paper and draw lots of small tickets with point values on them. You should be able to get about 48 on one sheet of paper. Get your sheet copied at a nearby instant printing store, library, or ask a parent if he or she can have it done at their office. Be sure to have enough tickets for all the booths—a couple of hundred should do. Reuse those that are turned in for prizes. The Head Barker should have extra tickets in his pocket when the carnival opens, just in case some booths run out.

Then you could have a "Prize Booth" where all the prizes are kept. Each prize should be marked with a certain number of points. The larger the

prize, the more points it takes to win it. Any time a customer wants to turn in the points that he won at all the different game booths, he can come to the Prize Booth and exchange them for a prize of that value.

Perhaps the club can select a committee to collect all the prizes. They should be sure of two things: 1) that all the prizes are in working order, and 2) that they have enough prizes on hand. What's left over can always be used at some other Kids-Only Club event.

Prizes at a backyard carnival need not be big or expensive. The fun is in the playing more than in the prize itself. Your club can get prizes in four ways:

1. Make the prizes. The next chapter has different craft items that you can put together yourself.

2. Or you can collect prizes from club members—old toys that still work, games you can still play, jigsaw puzzles with none of the pieces missing.

3. Buy prizes with money from the club treasury. You can get dozens of balloons, for example, for very little money. Small candy bars don't cost much either, and most toy stores have tiny toys which everyone would like to have. If you put more money into the prizes than you can make from the games, the treasury will lose money instead of make money.

Here's an example. If a prize cost the club 5¢, then to win it a player must pay *more* than 5¢. In fact, to win that prize the player should perhaps pay as much as 10¢. After all, the customer has the fun of playing the game, and that's worth something too.

4. See if somebody will give you prizes. Check with local toy and hobby stores. Sometimes, the store manager where you and the other club members buy things will give you some small prizes for your carnival. You can tell him you'll mention his name in your publicity as a prize contributor. If he won't give you anything free, he might sell some toys to you at a special low price.

There are other places to look for prizes. Try for a small "gift certificate" at your local ice cream store (good for one double-dip ice cream cone, for example). Other businesses (like hamburger stands and toy or hobby stores) also have them. The stores get advertising from the certificate and, besides, if winners come in with a free certificate, they may buy something too.

How about "secret sur-prizes"? What is a secret sur-prize? A secret sur-prize is a prize that you don't know anything about until after you pick it. Usually, the name of the prize is written on a piece of paper and put in a sealed envelope so no one can see what it is until the right moment. Here are some suggestions for sur-prizes: Try talking a club member's parents into offering to take the winner to the beach one day or to a local movie or amusement park or to a picnic.

Another sur-prize that you might give is a paper cup filled with planter's mix and a seed. The person who takes the prize home won't know for sure what he or she is getting until the seed sprouts. Be sure to attach watering instructions which you will find on the package in which the seeds come. Your local nursery can tell you the best seeds to grow in your area and how much light and water will be needed.

Building and Decorating the Booths

You don't need a hammer, saw, or carpenter to make booths for the games at your carnival. They're really simple to put together. You want them simple so they will be easy to put up and take down. Some booths can be just a pole or line, something to keep customers at a certain distance from the target. Other booths should have a shelf. Some can be made from a table. Here are three you can make with ease.

1. **A Broomstick Booth.** Place two light chairs or paper cartons a few feet apart from each other, then lay a broom or mop handle between them. Drape a cloth over the handle so that it reaches the ground. The cloth can be an old sheet, a bedspread, a tablecloth, a shower curtain, or even strips of crepe paper. A few staples or thumbtacks will hold the cloth in place. Be sure to use a cloth and chair you don't mind getting dirty.

2. **A Shelf Booth.** You will need to put rings and balls *on* some of the booths, so get large cardboard boxes from a store, and place them side by side until the booth is as large as you need. Use strong boxes, maybe even wooden ones (orange or apple crates), if you can get them. Cellophane tape or packing tape will hold the cardboard together. Some heavier tape or a few small nails will hold the

wooden boxes together. Tape a cloth over the whole works, and you will have a counter-type booth that will hold games and the things that go with them.

3. **A Card Table Booth.** A simple card table may be all you need for some of the games you want to play. A few strips of colored paper for decoration or a colorful cloth will do a lot to brighten it up for your carnival.

It Pays to Advertise

It would be a pity to give a carnival and have just a few people show up. That has happened to some groups, but it won't happen to yours if you get lots of publicity for your event, and get it early enough so that people will hear about it and make plans to attend.

Customers are important, so more than one club member should be responsible for getting out the publicity. The chapter on "Letting the World Know" will give you many ideas on how to let people know when and where your event is going to take place.

It also helps if each club member gets at least three friends outside the club to promise to come to the carnival. This will give you a "guaranteed" crowd. If you can get more, don't stop at three. If there's another club that you know about that you can invite (your brother's Scout troop, or your sister's class), why not have them come along too?

Barkers

The people who run the booths are called barkers. That's because they bark at the people passing by, telling them how much fun the game is to play. Some booths may need two club members to run them. At the time you test out each game, you'll know which ones need the extra helper.

Every event needs to be cleared away when it's over. Each barker can be responsible for his own booth. Then all of the barkers can work together with the Head Barker to clean up the backyard where the carnival was held. Have a couple of large plastic trash bags ready ahead of time for things you're going to throw away.

Carnival games are not played in a group. It is one person against the game itself. You win or lose the game by *yourself.*

All of the following games have been used by Scouts and kids' groups for years. You can make these games harder—or easier—whatever your Kids-Only Club wants to do. Add your own favorite games to this list too.

1. **Bean Jar.** One of the free games you could have at your carnival is a bean-guessing contest. Fill a large jar with beans (dry beans, please, not baked) and let everybody who comes guess how many are inside. The Head Barker should keep a record of each person's guess. At the end of the carnival, it's time to spill the beans. Do it in front of the crowd and count them out to see who the lucky winner is. Whoever comes closest to the number wins. If nobody (including the Head Barker) knows the total, he or she can guess too. To save time, you might want one person ahead of time to know the number of beans that were put in the jar, so you'll have the figure ready after all your customers have taken a guess.

2. **Knock over the Stack.** Use a broomstick booth for this easy game. The trick is to knock over all of the paper cups to win, not just most of them. Take two large paper plates and staple the edges together, face to face, to make a "flying disc." Now stack up a pyramid of 15 paper cup "pins." You make the "pins" by attaching two cups mouth to mouth with tape. Use five pins for the base of your pyramid, and place them about eight feet from the broomstick. Then stack four more on top, then three, two, and the last pin goes at the top.

Allow three throws of the disc (or make three discs) to tip over all of the cups. Award one point if all are tipped over; none if one or more of the cups are still standing.

Plastic detergent or bleach jars also make good targets if you fill them with water, and use a beanbag or soft ball (tossed *underhand)* to tip them. Use three jars stacked in a pyramid. To win, all three must be tipped on their sides.

3. **The Flying Saucer.** This game will work with a broomstick booth too. You need a disc made of two paper plates fastened together, as in the last game. The booth's barker might decorate the disc like a flying saucer with little windows.

About 20 feet away from the booth, make a 3-foot circle on the ground with brightly colored string or yarn, so it can be seen easily. The aim of the game is to land the saucer within the circle. Allow three throws of the disc to "land" it on target. Better yet, make three discs so that the "Flying Saucerer" can see his or her mistakes. If the disc lands in the circle, the player gets a point. If it doesn't, maybe the player might like to have three more tries for another nickel.

4. **Sink the Ship.** Some club member will have to bring a wading pool for this game. Get some styrofoam from a local department or variety store. This is sometimes thrown away so just ask if they have any extra before you buy it. Make rings from the styrofoam about 8 inches in diameter with 4-inch holes in the middle. Place the wading pool, filled with water, about 10 feet behind a broomstick booth and float the rings in the pool. The customer gets five ping-pong balls to toss into the rings. For every ball inside a ring, he or she might get a point.

5. **Feed the Cat.** This is an easy game with several ways to play it. Try any of them or try more than one at different booths. The game calls for a large hole in a paper plate. If you are using a plate with a design, turn it over and use the plain side. Draw the face of a cat around the hole, so that the hole becomes the cat's mouth. With two strings (so that it won't twist around) hang the cat face from a bush or branch of a tree or from a clothesline, about 10 feet behind a broomstick booth. Each customer gets five ping-pong balls to try to toss through the cat's mouth, winning a point for each ball that passes through.

You can "feed" your cat with other things too. Let customers make their favorite airplanes and try to fly them through the opening if they can.

Or make a picture of a clown's face on the side of a cardboard box. Cut the mouth area open and hang a bell there. Then try to throw a beanbag through the mouth so that the bag hits the bell.

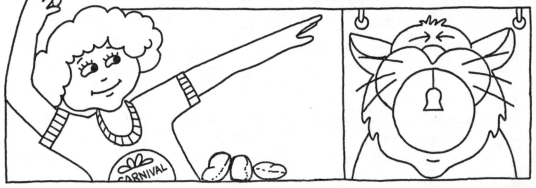

6. **Nail Driving.** Nail driving appeals to boys and girls alike. For this game you'll need a solid shelf (a wooden box or a small table), a piece of wood, and some long nails.

The person in charge pounds the nail first with a tap or two until it is standing up straight in the wood. Then the customer is allowed so many whacks to drive it all the way in. A customer under 10 should be allowed six whacks to drive the nail in. A customer over 10 should be allowed three whacks.

If a whack bends the nail, the customer is allowed to straighten it, but the whacks already used still count.

7. **Water Balloon or Sponge Toss.** This will be one of the most popular games on the midway, but you'll have to set things up ahead of time. And you'll need a willing assistant. About 25 feet behind a broomstick booth, set up one of the following things:

a. A large box turned on its side with a hole in it, with aluminum foil covering the front to make it waterproof, or

b. Two poles in the ground with a rope between and a plastic cloth hung over the rope, or

c. A kitchen chair and a raincoat or plastic poncho or tablecloth.

Have a boxful of small balloons filled with water, or a bucket of water and a bunch of kitchen sponges. A club member sticks his or her head out of the hole in the box. Or the head may be raised over the plastic cloth draped over the rope. Or the member can just put on a raincoat and sit in the chair. Each customer gets a balloon or a wet sponge to toss at the head. A hit gets a point and a cheer from the onlookers. A miss gets nothing but a lot of laughter and no doubt a sigh of relief from the one in the box.

The "target" ought to be allowed to move his or her head a little to avoid being hit but should never move out of the box or chair. Now you see why you need a *willing* assistant? Nobody wants to be a wet blanket, but . . .

8. **Box Golf.** Set up a series of boxes or pails separated by a few feet. The size of the yard and the size of the boxes will tell you how far apart they should be. The idea of this game is to throw a ball into each box in turn. (When you test this game, if a ping-pong or rubber ball bounces out all the time make some balls out of aluminum foil.) When players get the ball into one box, they can go on to the next one. If they get a ball into each box,

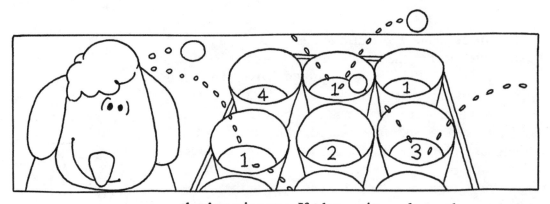

they're winners. If they miss a box, they are out.

9. **Cup Ball.** Stand paper cups in a tray made from a cut-down cardboard box. The larger the box you use, the more cups it will hold. In the bottom of each cup, mark a number from 1 to 5. Mark most of the cups with the number 1, and the others with a 2, 3, 4, 5. Scatter the higher numbered cups among the other cups.

Set the cup tray at a slight angle so the customer can see the numbers. Each player throws three ping-pong balls into the box and, of course, will aim for the high-numbered cups. Then watch the fun as the ping-pong ball bounces in and out and around.

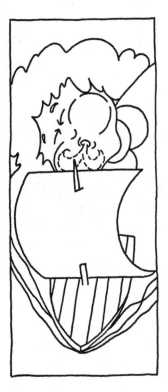

If you make a ramp (place a length of board from the ground to the bottom of the box) and the players *roll* the ball to the box instead of *tossing* it, you will have your own skeet ball game.

10. **Rain-Gutter Boat Race.** This one will need a little preparation, but it's a game everybody enjoys.

You need a 10-foot length of ordinary rain gutter of the type used on houses. Maybe one of the member's parents has a piece, or maybe you can buy or borrow a length from the local hardware or home improvement store. Plug each end with end caps. The same store should have these caps. What you have now is a long, narrow container which you will fill with water.

Give each customer a little 4-inch, boat-shaped piece of corrugated cardboard, a 3-by-5-inch card, and a toothpick. Scissors should be available for customers to cut sails of any size or shape they want. They attach the sail to the boat-shaped cardboard with the toothpick and launch their little ship from one end of the gutter.

They then blow the boat to the other end of the gutter. If it gets across within a certain time limit they win. Otherwise, all they do is have a lot of fun. If it's a windy day, you might have a lot of winners.

11. **Hole in the Cup Ball.** This game is like basketball, only on a much smaller scale. Make up quite a few small aluminum foil balls. Remove the bottom from a large paper cup and attach it upright with a small nail or thumbtack to a tree, a wall, or a couple of cardboard boxes piled on top of each other.

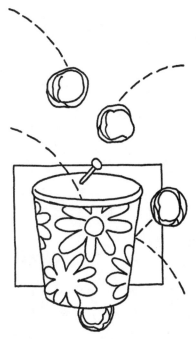

Customers are put behind a broomstick booth and given five foil balls each. For every ball tossed through the paper cup basket, give one point. This is not an easy game, so don't put the cup more than five feet from the player.

12. **Ring Toss.** All you need for this game are a few paper plates with the center cut out, pennies taped around the edges to give it extra weight, and a kitchen chair turned on its side. Label each chair leg with different points. Let players stand behind a broomstick booth. Give each player three rings to toss onto the legs. Decide ahead of time what total number of points makes your customer a winner.

13. **Marble Roll.** A shoebox works best for this easy game. You'll also need a smooth surface

about four feet across (a plank, a card table top, a cardboard carton top, etc.) on which to put the shoebox. Cut the box, as shown, with the larger tunnels worth only one point, and the smaller openings worth five points, but be sure a marble can actually roll through. The idea of the game is to roll five marbles through the openings in the box. If the marble bounces off, it still counts as one roll. To figure the score, add the player's total number of points.

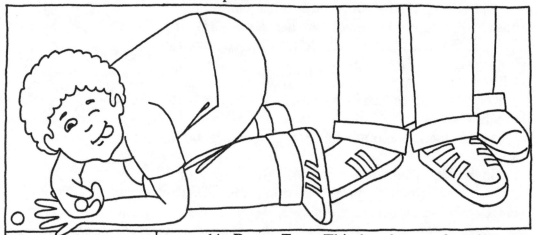

14. **Penny Toss.** This has been a favorite pasttime at grown-up carnivals for many, many years. Fill a large tub with water. Then in the middle submerge a round fish bowl (or any bowl or curved dish, open at the top) where it can be seen by the player. Players stand behind a broomstick booth about three or four feet away and try to toss pennies right into the sunken bowl.

It looks easy. But it isn't. The water makes the pennies slip and slide and drift around, and only a few will get into the bowl. Give a point for each penny that does get in. Put no limit on the number of tosses, since your club collects all the pennies in the *bottom* of the tub for your treasury.

For this game, you can use your "sense" ahead of time, and make sure you have a bunch of cents on hand for everybody who needs change.

15. **Roping Contest.** Make a bull's head out of a couple of pieces of wood nailed together. Or you can tape together four or five layers of cardboard from grocery boxes and cut them into the shape of a bull's head. Stick the head on a wooden stake in the ground and see if the local cowboys can rope your "steer" for points. A piece of clothesline will serve as your lasso. You don't want to give your players a "bum steer" but if you add horns, it will be harder—but not impossible—for the winner to get the rope over the bull's head.

16. **Go Fish.** Give customers a chance to catch a clothespin "fish." Float some clothespins in a tub of water. Be sure to use old-fashioned, wooden clothespins. They're the only kind that float. Attach a string to a pole, tie a nut—not a peanut, a nut and bolt nut—on the end, and see how many clothespin fish the players can hook out of the tub.

You can do this without water too. Make your hook from a coat hanger wire or a paper clip. Instead of clothespins, make the fish out of wood, cardboard, or paper cups. Hammer or push one nail through each, then drop all the fish into the tub. When players hook onto the nail in the "fish" and lift it out of the "pond," they will rate high not only as pretty fair fishermen, but earn themselves a couple of points as well.

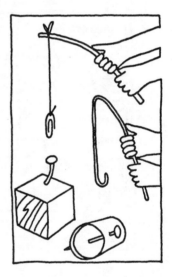

17. **Miss 'Em.** This one is especially great for those who have trouble with their aim. In most games you need to hit the target or knock something down. The point of this game is just the opposite. You're supposed to *miss.*

Set up 8 or 10 bottles, tin cans, or paper cups, so that you've got an obstacle course through which customers must roll a marble (or marbles) without touching any of the bottles, cans, or cups. Give your customers three chances to see if they can steer clear of all the targets. You can't miss with this game.

Chapter 9
Craft-Making and Giving Craft Fairs

A craft fair is two-way fun. First, you have the fun of making things, then you get the kick of having a fair to show others how to make them—for their pleasure and your profit.

The only difference between a carnival and a craft fair is the type of booths you need. At a carnival you had games. At a craft fair you will have things to make and things to sell. So follow the plan in the last chapter on how to set up a carnival.

A craft fair, too, takes planning and person power. Someone will have to make arrangements for the place where you'll have the craft fair, and committees must be picked to arrange for the booths and craft materials. Club members in charge of each booth could build and decorate their own, as the club did for the carnival. Then those same members could run their own booths on Craft Fair Day. Somebody should be in charge of getting publicity with posters and press releases. Everything from opening up to cleaning up should be planned in advance.

Here are some suggestions for different kinds of booths for your craft fair and the crafts you can make or teach at each of them. Be sure to have booths for your own favorite crafts too.

1. A "Free" Booth
2. Hands-On Booths
3. A Photo Booth
4. A Flying Things Booth
5. A Living Things Booth
6. A Things "For-Sale" Booth

Each booth can be decorated with many samples that you have made of the finished item that kids will put together in that booth. In this way you'll be showing how nice the craft or activity

looks and also give the customer some examples that he or she might wish to follow.

For many of the craft booths you will need odd scraps of material, colored paper, bits of broken jewelry, all sizes of buttons, sequins, feathers, gift cards, or old wrapping paper, and other things that might be amusing when used as part of a decoration. As soon as you have decided to put on a craft fair, get each member of your club to start collecting shoeboxes or bags full of these things, so that when the day comes for your fair, you'll have more than enough on hand without dipping into your treasury.

To start the fun and warm people up to your fair, set up a Free Booth at the very entrance.

A "Free" Booth

Everybody likes something for nothing. Besides, these are things that get people into the spirit of the fair, and it is possible some kids attending your fair may not have any money at all,

and it would be a shame to make them feel unwelcome.

Of course, anything you give away shouldn't cost you much in the first place or else the club treasury will be hurt.

Here are a few inexpensive, lively things that kids will want to make and use.

1. **Moustaches.** Actors, detectives, and secret agents all know that no other disguise can change the way a person looks as fast as a moustache can. Both boys and girls like to wear them, too. Get some heavy colored paper. Give each kid a cardboard shape to trace, a pencil, and a pair of scissors. The little loops fit into the nose and hold the moustache in place. If you can get every boy or girl who comes to your fair to make and wear a moustache, soon everybody will be walking around smiling, ready to have fun.

2. **Greeting Cards.** Before the craft fair, your club should collect a lot of old greeting cards. Put them in a box or pile them on the booth, along with some scissors, white glue, and colored construction paper that is cut in half and then folded double. Give each customer one folded paper, let him pick a greeting card and cut out the pretty figures on the card. Now the front of the colored sheet is covered with white glue, and the cut figures are pasted on the construction paper any way that looks best. For a final touch, the entire front of the card is covered with a thin layer of white glue. This gives an old, lovely finish to your new, very original card.

This is also a good way for Kids-Only Club members to make cards for Christmas or any other holiday. Recycling old cards helps nature, saves money, and cheers up friends who get one of these one-of-a-kind greetings.

3. **Drinking Straw Whistles.** Kids love noise. When it's tuneful, it's even better. Here's a noisemaker, called a Drinking Straw Whistle, you can give away free. That should put people in a good mood and they can really sound off.

Give each customer an ordinary plastic drinking straw. Flatten it at one end and crease it so it will stay flat. Then cut the flat end into a "V" shape with scissors. The customer puts the V end into his or her mouth, and blows. Be sure to tell them not to press down on the V with their lips, otherwise nothing will happen. You can change the sound of the whistle by changing the length of the straw.

Hands-On Booths

For these booths, have plenty of materials on hand, so that you don't run out of things before your craft fair is really underway. Anything leftover can be used by club members at a later time.

Make sure your club charges different prices for the different craft booths. This way any kid with just a few dimes in his pocket can still find things to make or do. Since most of the materials you collect will either be free or cost you very little money, make sure that your club doesn't charge the customers too much.

Here's a way to figure out prices: Figure out how much the material to make each craft cost you. Then add another 10¢ or 15¢ for your club's profit. That should be the amount you charge.

Be sure you make at least one of every item before the fair. This will do two things: 1) It will give you things to display in the booths, and 2) it will prepare you to show customers how to do the craft when they come to your booth and say, "Hey, I'd like to try that."

For the things they'd like to try, read on.

1. **Happy Turtle Paperweight Booth.** For each turtle, you will need a smooth, round rock, a few ice-cream spoons, a little glue, and paint. Find the rocks at the beach, along a stream, or in the woods. You might even buy the rocks. They don't cost much at a building supply store or nursery. Or perhaps you can get them free in exchange for a sign at that booth which says: "All stones from the 'So & So' Building Supply Store." They should be flat on the

bottom and rounded on top. This will be the turtle's "house." Have ready poster paints in paper cups and cotton swabs for the "house painting."

Customers can draw on some fancy designs, or even put some lettering on it like "Rock Hudson." Then they paint the spoons green and attach them to the bottom of the rock with glue. Add eyes to the spoon sticking out in front.

These little paperweights are sure to be an "I want to make one too" success story when your customers see how cute the ones are that line your booth. You can also make them without feet. They'll still hold down paper. They're not going anywhere anyway, except into a customer's home and desk.

2. **Flower Stationery Booth.** To make this craft, you will need a large assortment of "book-dried" flowers and other little greens, leaves, and plants. Collect pretty flowers (flatter ones are better than bulky ones) and press them in books between wax paper until they are dry. This will take a few days. With a supply of pressed flowers, you can have a booth where your customers will stand in line to make a sheet of "Flower Stationery" which they can take away in a matching envelope.

For the stationery, get a supply of ordinary white typing paper, and cut each sheet in half. Fold each of these half sheets in half once again. Buy inexpensive envelopes. Trim the stationery to fit the envelopes you've bought, but don't do the trimming from the folded edge. Arrange the flowers on the top edge or along the fold. Glue them in place, using ordinary white glue. Or you can glue a strip of colored construction paper across the top or down the side. Then glue the flowers on this strip.

Place a sheet of waxed paper over the whole thing, and tell your customer to put it in a book to dry overnight. Each sheet of stationery will be slightly different, and each will be totally unique, with a helping hand from Mother Nature.

3. **Sand Jar and Sand Painting Booth.** Sand pouring is fascinating. To prepare for your booth, you'll need paper cups, fine sand, food coloring, and small glass jars with lids (empty jelly jars are nice). Work out of doors or in the kitchen. Fill each paper cup about three-quarters full with sand. Then cover the sand with water to which you have added food coloring or fabric dye. Stir to get the colored water and sand thoroughly mixed. The more color you add, the darker the sand will be. After about 15 minutes, punch a small hole in the bottom of each cup and let the water drain out. Be careful. Do this over the sink. Then spread each cup of sand on a sheet of newspaper and let the sand dry completely. Each stack will now be a different color.

When the sand is dry, store in fresh paper cups or large jars.

In your booth, have the customer spoon a layer into the bottom of a glass jar. Then spoon another layer of a different color carefully on top of the first layer. Don't shake the jar. Keep adding layers of colored sand until the last layer reaches almost to the top of the jars.

Use a wire (an open paper clip or a straightened hanger) to punch down along the inside of the jar through all the layers of sand. As you take the wire out, a pretty design is made in the sand. Then fill the last little bit of space at the top and seal the jar. The Sand Jar can now be moved without disturbing the fascinating design.

A second sandy activity is Sand Painting. Provide white glue, paper, and colored sand. (See above for instructions on how to color the sand.) Your customer draws a design on a piece of paper, then "paints" in the designs one section at a time with white glue. (Thin the glue with a little water if it is too thick to paint with.) Sprinkle on the color of sand that you want. The next section is "painted" with glue and sprinkled with colored sand in the same way. The result will be a beautiful sand painting. Once the glue is dry, the sand will stick to where it was poured. Meantime, your customer can go to another booth. When dry, turn it over and tap away any excess sand so the painting won't leak sand on everything later. Dried (used) coffee grounds, rice, salt, and pepper work in the same way too.

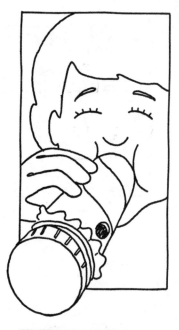

4. **Kazoo Booth.** Give each customer a paper tube that comes from inside a roll of toilet paper or any other short piece of cardboard tube, such as that from a roll of paper towels. They will also need a rubber band and a piece of wax paper. Aluminum foil will also work, but the tone of the kazoo will be much higher. The customer wraps the paper or foil around the end of the tube, then fastens it in place with the rubber band. Be sure the paper is stretched tightly across the end. Now with a pencil punch a hole at that end of the tube about one inch from the wrapping.

If you put the open end of the tube over your mouth, pucker your lips, and sing or hum a tune, you'll get a real old-fashioned kazoo sound. Keep trying till you get the hang of it. Now you can make music wherever you go. That's more than a piano player can do.

5. **Foam Funnies Booth.** If all your Kids-Only clubbers ask their parents to save the styrofoam blobs that come in packages from department stores, you should have several bagsful by the day of your fair. Each customer gets, say, 10 lumps of foam, three pipe cleaners, and a pair of scissors. Have felt-tipped pens on the table too. Cut the pipe cleaners into various lengths and stick them into the foam shapes, and animals, cars, chairs, space ships, and many other wonderful things will suddenly appear from the shapes.

6. **Wood Things Booth.** This is the most popular booth at lots of Boy Scout fairs. Have a box of small hardwood scraps, free of splinters, from

the local cabinet or carpenter shop or lumberyard. Workers will probably save such scraps for you and give them to you free to use at your fair.

You provide white glue and Q-tips to apply it. Then watch the amazing items your customers will make: planes, odd-looking houses, animals. If you have felt-tip pens on hand, customers can draw eyes, doors, or designs on the wood to add to their pleasure.

7. **Design Board Booth.** From your local lumber dealer get scrap wood about a foot square, ½- to ¾-inch thick. Shapes other than squares will do too.

Give your customer some nails with heads on them and a hammer, and let him or her pound nails into the board in any design, leaving about ½ inch of the nail sticking out. Then provide yarn, string, rubber bands, even thin strips of fabric, which the customer will connect from one nail to another. The "picture" made can be very geometric or without any special pattern at all. Either way, the banging and the stringing are lots of fun. It's the best way to string along a pal.

This craft sometimes uses up yards of string, so be sure to get a very inexpensive kind if you are buying it. It would be great if you could get colored string or color it yourself by unraveling the ball before the fair and dyeing it in a vegetable coloring.

8. **A Puppet and Mask Booth.** Making easy puppets and masks is perfect for craft fairs. To keep your materials low in cost, use paper cups and paper bags.

Some of the puppets described in the "Doing a Puppet Show" chapter and the masks from the "Putting On a Play" chapter can all be made quickly at a booth. If you are going to make puppets, have ready a basic pattern for the paper "sleeve" to go around the cup or precut a lot of sleeves for your customers.

You might also provide a box of large tissues and rubber bands so they can make simple "bodies" as well. Next to your puppet booth you could set up a simple puppet stage so that anybody who wants to can get behind the carton and have his or her puppets talk to people passing by. A little free entertainment never hurt.

If your Kids-Only Club members collect and bring paper bags from home, customers can also try easy-to-make puppets. The illustration will show you how to hold them and where to put your hand.

9. **God's Eye Booth.** When you learn how to make these yourself, you'll have no trouble teaching the kids who come to your booth.

Use twigs, pencils, cotton swab sticks, or any kind of thin rods. Unroll about two feet of a ball of wool and lay it straight out on a table. Put the two sticks next to each other across the wool, and tie a single knot around the middle of both. Pull it very tight, then tie another knot over the first.

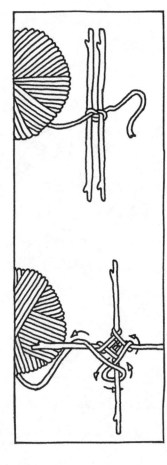

Twist the sticks so that they cross one another to form a giant cross. Pinch the center of the cross between your thumb and pointer finger, and wind both strands of wool (the one connected to the ball and the short leftover end) around one stick (right next to the knot where the sticks cross). Then stretch your double strand over to the next stick to the right.

Shift the position of your thumb and pointer finger so that you can easily wrap the strand over, under, and around this next stick on your cross. Now stretch the strand across to the third stick, always moving in the same direction (it's a good idea to keep winding the wool clockwise). As you wind the yarn around the sticks, keep adjusting your hold on the cross of sticks so that the stick around which you are wrapping is always nearest you, pointing in your general direction.

Soon you will have used up the short end of the yarn and will only be wrapping a single strand around the sticks. Keep winding in this way until your design is the right size.

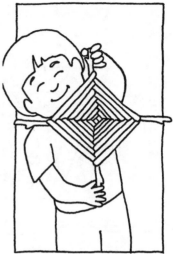

To change colors in the middle of your design, stick the strand you're working with securely between stitches in the back. Then insert the beginning of the next color of wool under some other stitches in the back and continue winding in the same way. You might like to let the knobby ends of the twigs or the little white cotton puffs of the swabs extend past your design, or you may prefer to wind right to the ends with the wool. When you've gone as far as you wish, cut your yarn and wedge the loose end between some of the stitches in the back of your design.

If you want your wool wound right to the very end, dab each of the four stick ends with a glue that dries clear and transparent or with a blob of shellac.

10. **An Egg Decoration Booth.** For this one club members will need the cooperation of their parents for a few weeks before the fair. What the club needs is dozens of empty eggshells which can then be decorated into egg people and puppets.

It would be nice to have the chicken cooperate too, but we haven't found a way yet to get them to lay empty eggshells so get your parents to let you empty all of the eggs used in your house the following way: With a needle, poke a hole in each end of the shell. Then blow through one end, and the egg will come plopping out the other. It's hard to believe but that's what really happens. Wash the inside of the shell thoroughly by running water through the two openings, and set your empty eggshells aside to dry out. Save them in an empty egg carton and they will not break.

For your booth also collect ends of fabric, ribbon, string, tiny buttons, sequins, feathers, scraps of colored paper, cotton, bits of broken jewelry, boxes of all shapes, paper cups, excelsior

from gift boxes, paper doilies, crayons or ink pen, colored plastic tape, cellophane tape, rubber cement, blunt scissors.

Now customers can cut and paste the odds and ends to the egg form. For the display your club might make a whole egg circus or an egg football team.

You can also turn an egg into a puppet. Just make the hole at the bottom large enough to fit over your pointer finger. Drape a napkin over your hand for the body, or use a paper cup with a hole in the bottom to poke your finger through into the hole of your egg head.

A Photo Booth

Many families now have instant picture cameras, and if you want to spend a little money on film you can make a little money if you set up a photo booth at your craft fair. You should earn your money back and then some if you take snapshots of people attending the fair and put them in frames you made ahead of time.

Some kids may want a candid shot of themselves and their friends as they walk or stand around at the fair. This kind of unposed picture is quick to shoot.

If you want to get a little fancier, find a large cardboard box and cut a hole in the front of it through which your customers can stick their heads. Then paint the front of the box so that the customer's head is on top of the funny body, a snake or a flower, and he or she will have a silly photo with which to remember the afternoon.

It's the frames that will make this booth a success. Make them up ahead of time, add the picture you just took, and your fair customer can take away the finished product without waiting.

Here are three frames for you to try.

1. For this frame you'll need four twigs: two of one size and two of another. Lay the short twigs across the top and bottom of the larger ones, then

tie them together with stout cord. To make it extra strong, glue them where they are tied. Cut a piece of colored construction paper to fit the frame. Glue in place on the backs of the twigs. Now cut out a window slightly smaller than the size of the picture you will take. When you get the picture, tape it in place in the window you have cut.

2. To make a shell frame, cut a square of heavy cardboard. Then cut a hole in the center of the square which is slightly smaller than the instant picture. Glue shells all around the frame. Add the picture you take at the fair.

3. Another very pretty frame can be made with tiny twigs glued to a cardboard frame like the one described above. Break the twigs into ½- or ¾-inch pieces, glue them in place, so they overlap one another. Branches from small trees or bushes will do. But be sure to pick them off the ground, not off living trees.

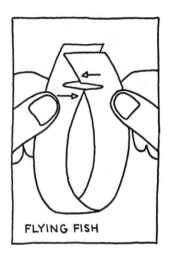

FLYING FISH

A Flying Things Booth

It may take a little experimentation to get some of these flying things to work just right, but the Wright brothers didn't get off the ground the first time either. Make them first yourself. Find the best method of launching. Then when you open up your airport booth, you'll be off to a flying start, with no crash landings.

1. **Flying Fish.** This is such fun. Take a strip of paper. Cut a slit at the upper end on one side. Cut another slit at the lower end on the opposite side. Bring the two ends together and fit one slit into the other to form a paper loop. Now toss it high into the air and watch it whirl its way to the ground.

2. **Twirling Helicopter.** All you need is one long, narrow strip of paper, folded in half. Bend one top end down to the right, the other down to the left. Put a paper clip over the bottom fold. Toss it high into the air and watch it twirl.

3. **Pocket Parachute.** Take an ordinary plastic bag or any plastic sheet (plastic works better than

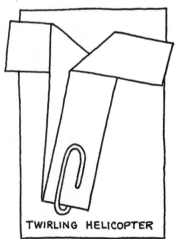

TWIRLING HELICOPTER

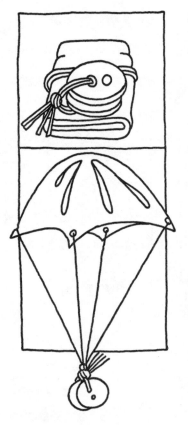

cloth for parachutes because it is light yet strong). Cut it into a 12-inch square. Let your customer make a hole in each corner with a pencil point (not too close to the edge), then tie a 12-inch long piece of string to each hole. Take the ends of all four strings and tie where they meet into one big knot. To this knot, tie a weight. You can use a couple of washers, a bundle of 15 paper clips, a few heavy old buttons, etc. Fold the parachute neatly as shown and throw it into the air.

4. **Paper Planes.** People love to make paper planes. Most people have a special design they think is best. Why not have your Flying Things Booth supply paper of different thicknesses and sizes, paper clips, and glue so customers make their favorites? A box of crayons to decorate these planes will make them even more colorful. Once they design their own, they can show off just how well they fly at the "airport" right next to the booth. You can even run a contest to judge distance, accuracy, and the length of time the plane stays in the air. Look out for the jumbo jets.

A Living Things Booth

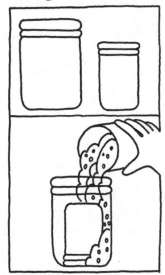

Besides making things, people like to watch things happen. Here are some suggestions for a booth for just such people where living things are sold.

1. **Ant Jar.** Anybody who has one of these can watch ants build a maze of tunnels and carry food to their underground home. Make as many as you can, for these will sell very well at your fair. By making them in advance and keeping the ants alive, you can be sure that you are selling a healthy colony to your customers.

You'll need two clear glass jars for each ant jar, one slightly smaller than the other, and some sandy soil for the ants to build their homes in. Put the smaller jar upside down inside the larger jar, then fill the space between the two jars with sandy soil. Don't pack it tight.

If you can't find an ant hill nearby, be a small-game hunter and trap some by putting a small jar or can on its side with some sugar-water inside. Make sugar-water by dissolving a table-spoonful of sugar in a half cup of water. The ants will come for "dinner" and you'll have the ants. Or just dig up part of an ant hill from your yard or nearby park or empty lot.

You'll need about 20 ants for each ant jar, all from the same hill, otherwise they'll fight. Put the ants in the jar and screw on the lid. The fewer the ants, the more active they'll be. Don't worry about punching holes for air. When you remove the lid to add food, plenty of air will go in.

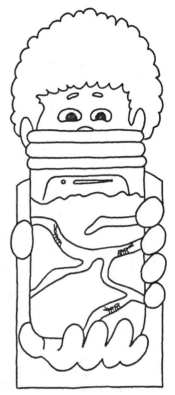

Once each week (no more) feed the ants about four drops of sugar water, maybe a birdseed or two, or a tiny crumb of bread. If you don't shake the jar and disturb them, they'll build a complete city inside. Be sure to give feeding instructions when you sell your ant friends. They'll appreciate it.

2. **Growing Plants.** For more excitement, watching what happens to a planted seed is hard to beat. There's one trouble—most seeds grow underground where nobody can see them when they break open and send a root down while the sprout works up towards the light. But here are some ways you can show the mystery to everybody and at the same time attract attention to your Living Things Booth at the fair:

a. Stick some toothpicks through a sweet pota-to, beet, onion, or garlic. Then suspend it halfway into a glass or jar of water. Allow about two weeks, and then things will start happening from both ends. Roots will grow down from the vegetable into the water, and soon sprouts pop up from the top.

b. For another attention-getter, roll up a flat kitchen sponge and put it in a glass so that it presses against the sides. Add enough water to soak the sponge, but not so much that it sinks to the bot-tom. Stick some seeds between the sponge and the

glass. Corn, squash, or kidney bean seeds are best, as are flower, apple, lemon, or orange seeds. Then, in a few days, things like roots start going down and shoots go shooting up.

c. You can also have living, growing plants in coffee can planters for sale at your Living Things Booth. You can make a number of these before the craft fair begins. Take an empty, one-pound coffee can (the kind with a plastic top) and with an ordinary can opener, punch four drainage holes in the bottom of the can. To prevent rusting, spray the inside with clear acrylic paint. Allow a few minutes to dry, then spray paint the outside a bright and cheery color. When dry, take a package of decals and paste them to the painted can. Once you've added your soil, seed or plant, put the plastic top on the *bottom* of the can, and you've got a great indoor planter. When you water, remove the plastic bottom to allow the water to drain from the holes. When drained completely, put the plastic back on again.

Now that you've got a fancy planter, get some not-so-fancy plants at a nearby nursery where they will also help you with the planting if you need it. Buy the sturdiest plants they have. Small ones are good because they don't cost much. Get instructions for keeping them alive: how often to water and what kind of light they need. Print this on a card and attach it to your planter so that your customers will know what to do to keep their new green friends healthy and happy. What you don't sell, take home and enjoy yourself.

A Things "For Sale" Booth

If any of the members of your club are really good at making something—perhaps jewelry or model airplanes, knitting, crocheting, macrame or growing indoor plants, you might have A Things "For Sale" Booth. Of course, you must have items that people are going to want to buy, so let your club think about this carefully so you will know if a booth of this kind will really work for you. It may turn out that people who come to your craft fair would rather make their own items than buy yours. If this happens, remember you already had the fun of making them anyway, and now you can enjoy the things you made yourself or give them away as gifts.

Chapter 10
Throwing Parties for Fun and Profit

You know how to give a terrific party for yourself. You know what you like to do. Games you like to play. Foods that say "party" to you. The music, dancing, decorations that set the right mood for any party get-together. So you probably don't need any suggestions about party-giving for your club members.

But imagine how many people in your neighborhood would be interested if your club offered to put on a party for their little children—from beginning to end. All the parent would have to do is make and serve the food. Your club would take care of the invitations, decorations, games, favors—everything.

Most parents would pay good dollars for this service, and they would pick up all of the expenses as well. And would it be fun for your club!

Parents are usually interested in either birthday, Christmas, or Halloween parties at their home. The ideas in this chapter can be used for any of those occasions. And you can use all of these tips to put on your own club parties as well.

To put on any kind of a party, think about:
1. Advance planning
2. Invitations
3. Decorations
4. Party hats and favors
5. Games
6. Clean-up

Advance Planning

Make up a flyer—a single sheet of paper to let your neighbors know about your party service. This should announce that your Kids-Only Club gives parties for little children and provides the invitations, decorations, games, etc. Don't forget to list some club members' phone numbers so that your future customers know whom to call. Then make copies of your flyer and slip them under the door of every home with kids in your area.

When your first call comes in, arrange for a Party Committee to meet with the parents and tell them what your club will do and what you expect to be paid. The parents will tell you the kind of party they want to have, the date, time, and location.

Before you say, "Yes," check with other club members to be sure there will be enough people to help run the party on the chosen day. Then decide with the parents how long the party will last. Suggest that the food be served near the end of the party and have only one or two activities afterward. It's best to have the party end while everyone is still having a good time and before the kids get too tired. Then make your plans and stick to them.

The important thing for you to remember is that parties for young children should be simple. They needn't be fancy because kids love action and are always *ready* to have fun. But they do need to be organized, to be watched, and helped with their games. That's where your Kids-Only Club comes in.

Most of the activities from other parts of this book can be used to put on a great party. The games from the "Running a Carnival" chapter might work very well for you. The puppet play or magic show could fascinate the little kids. And you may find that making easy puppets is the perfect quiet activity right after the food is served. Many of the crafts from the craft fair chapter will also be fun for the partygoers. Just remember that you are dealing with children smaller than you are and that some of the things that are easy for you may be difficult for them.

Invitations

A party for younger children should include only about 10 kids. They should all be about the same age so that the games and activities will appeal to everyone. The parents should give you the names and addresses of the kids they want to invite, but be sure the birthday boy or girl is asked about this too.

Your club will take care of the inviting, but let the parents give you the stamps for mailing. Postage is expensive, and your club wants to make money on this party.

Here is a funny suggestion for an invitation.

A Bal-looney Invitation. Blow up a balloon, but don't tie the knot. Write out the invitation right on the balloon with a felt-tipped pen. The invitation should tell who is having the party, when, where, and why. Put what time the party starts and ends, so the parents pick up the kids promptly once it is over. Now let the air out of the balloon, stick it in an envelope with a note attached saying, "Blow me up for a surprise," and mail or hand deliver it. The little child who gets it will have the fun of getting the invitation and then playing with it.

A red balloon invitation would be nice at Christmas, and an orange "pumpkin-y" one would be just the right color for a Halloween party.

Other original cards for invitations are described in the chapter, "Craft-Making and Giving Craft Fairs."

The more complicated you make the party decorations, the harder it is to clean up later. The easiest idea, and in many ways the prettiest and most amusing for the children, is to plan to make as many of your decorations out of balloons as possible. Balloons are colorful. Balloons say "fun" to children. They lend themselves to a wide variety of decoration. Best of all, they're not expensive and the kids can take them home.

A centerpiece made out of a decorated balloon to suit the day is a good way to give the table a party look. If yours is a Christmas party, make a Balloon Santa. For Halloween, create a Balloon-O-Lantern. For birthdays, make it a Balloon Indian or just a Balloon-Funny of your own design.

Here are some simple ways to decorate balloons:

For Bal-loonies, you will need scissors, a large paper cup (the wider the base the better), crayons, cellophane tape, rubber band, balloons. Decorate a paper cup to look like the body of whatever kind of figure you want to draw. (See "Doing a Puppet Show" chapter for decorating paper cups.) Make a small hole in the bottom of the cup. Blow up your balloon, decorate it, and tie a rubber band around the knot. Place the balloon above the hole on top of the cup, and pull the rubber band down through that hole and tape it in place in the bottom of the cup. To finish up this charming fellow, all you need to do is tape the rubber band to the inside of the cup, and his head will remain firmly in place.

Balloon-O-Lantern. You will need a round orange balloon, scissors, black plastic tape or black construction paper, rubber cement, string or box, crepe paper (optional), thread (optional).

Inflate the balloon and tie a knot. Decide whether the pumpkin is to be hung in a doorway or from the ceiling fixture with tape, or placed in the middle of the table. If it is to be hung, make your pumpkin face with the knot on top. If it is to be

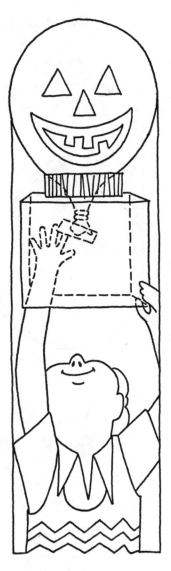

"tabled," put the knot on the bottom. Cut two eyes, a nose, and mouth out of plastic tape or construction paper. The shape is up to you. Then stick the features to the orange balloon with tape, glue, or rubber cement.

To hang your pumpkin, tie a string to the knot on top of the balloon. To sit the pumpkin in the center of your party table, use a box of any kind as a base. Make a tiny hole in the center of the top of the box and, holding the balloon above the box, pull the knot through the hole. Tape the knot in place inside the box.

If you wish, the pumpkin can be surrounded by a "collar" of crepe paper. Just run a row of huge stitches down the middle of the strip of crepe paper. Then pull the thread until the strip is gathered into a ruffle. Circle the balloon with the paper ruffle and tape it in position.

Make more of these funny balloon creatures to fit the special kind of party you are giving. Hang them around the room. Then when you are playing games with the children, you can divide your company into two groups. Relay fashion, have each group carry its Balloon-Funny on a tablespoon from a starting line to a point across the room and then back again. No, it's not too easy, because every time the balloon drops, the child must pick it up and go back to the starting line.

With plenty of balloons, some rubber cement, string, cellophane tape, paper cups and plates, cotton balls, construction paper, and odds and ends of wool and fabric scraps, you can make Balloon-Anythings that will colorfully — and inexpensively— decorate any party.

At party's end maybe some of the kids will want to take your decorations home. That's a great way to tell people about your party-giving service.

If your party is a seasonal one (Christmas, Easter, or Halloween) go through magazines that month, and cut out witches and goblins, Santa

Clauses and Christmas trees, Easter bunnies and Easter eggs. You can hang these paper cutouts as party decorations if you paste them first on construction paper and then cut them out. This gives them a colorful "backing." Or you can glue these paper cutouts to party hats you make (see the next section). You can also glue them to paper cups to use as candy cups on the party table.

You and your Kids-Only Club members can hang the party decorations an hour before the guests arrive. But everything should be ready ahead of time, so that the decorating will be easy to do on the day of the party.

Remember to remove all knick-knacks and other breakables from the party area.

If some of the games you are planning require a set-up, this is the time to do that too.

Party Hats

Everybody loves funny hats at a party, even grownups! You can get your party off to a super start by trying some of the following ideas:

A Do-It-Yourself Hat Bar is a nice way to begin. Set up a table with crayons, bits of crepe paper, feathers, lengths of ribbon, string, yarn, small balloons, colored paper, scissors, glue, etc., and a bunch of paper plates and paper cups. When each youngster comes in, the club member who is supervising that table helps the kids to make and decorate their own hats. Then when everyone has arrived, you can give a prize for the prettiest or funniest hat (let the guests vote). In making hats there are no rules, except that they stay on the head most of the time. Try these.

Be-a-Bunny-or-a-Mouse Hat. For each hat you will need one big paper plate, two long balloons (for a bunny) or two small round ones (for a mouse), two 8-inch pieces of string or ribbon. Make two small slits on the paper plate, one on each side, directly opposite each other. Inflate the balloon under the plate, "ears" will float above, and you'll

63

have a bunny or a mouse depending on the size. Tie a knot at the end of each string and wedge one string into each of the same two slits. This time though the knot goes on top, and the string hangs below the plate. The plate is placed on the child's head and the string or ribbon tied under the chin. This hat will make each little guest look as cute as Peter Rabbit or Mickey or Minnie Mouse.

The Simplest and the Best. Wonderful party hats can be made out of large paper plates. Cut a slot from the edge of the plate to the center. Overlap the two flaps of the slit, and you will have a pointed cone. A nice big piece of tape or a staple gun will hold the cone in shape. This will be the start of making absolutely sensational party hats. Decorate each hat in a different way, so that every child at the party will feel very "special."

Try making a small paper fan by accordion-pleating a tiny square of paper. Tape it right to the point of the hat. Gift-wrapping paper is very good for this kind of decoration.

Make a ruffle around the brim of your pointed paper-plate hat. Apply a 1-inch band of glue or rubber cement around the bottom edge of the outside area of the cone. Crinkle up a strip of crepe paper. Press it into the glue any way you want all around the base of the hat.

Save leftover bows from gift packages all through the year. Tape a bow (the bigger the better) to the tip of the pointed hat or at the front of it.

Make up your own decorations for these pointed paper plate hats, according to the occasion. Christmas jingle bells strung on bits of wool are fun. Designs cut from old greeting cards or magazines pasted smack in front of the hat are also colorful.

Party Favors

One way to make sure little kids have a good time is to have them go home with their arms full of "loot." Here are a few things that are easy

64

and inexpensive for you to make, but great fun for them to have.

Pop-Up Puppets. You will need paper cups, drinking straws, old gift wrap or construction paper, glue or tape.

Here's what to do: Draw a puppet face on a piece of construction paper. Or cut the face of a fireman, an animal, a goblin, ghost, witch, bunny, Santa Claus, or anything else out of a magazine. But the face has to be small— small enough to fit inside a paper cup. Glue or tape this little cut-out face to one end of a drinking straw. Now decorate the outside of each paper cup. Then with the end of a pencil, poke a hole in the bottom of the cup. Stick in the straw from the inside of the cup. When the child pushes the straw up and down, the puppet will play peek-a-boo, hide-and-seek, and rise and fall, and come and go.

The heads for your puppets can also be made out of eggshells (see the Egg Decorating Booth in "Running a Carnival").

Place Cards. These are little signs you can put at each place at the table to show the kids where they sit.

Surprise Favor. Here's a place card that's also a favor. Have club members save the cardboard tubes from bathroom tissue rolls. Fill each tube with wrapped candy, then place it on some gift wrapping paper or brightly colored tissue paper. Roll the tube in the paper and twist the ends. Then tie each end with a ribbon and attach a name tag onto one of these ribbons.

A Tastier Place Card. Stand a lollypop into a large gumdrop or poke the lollypop through a hole into the bottom of an upside-down paper cup. Attach a paper "flag" with the child's name on it to the lollypop stick.

Games

What's a party without games? Not much fun, as you know. You will want to play several, so plan them ahead. Of course, warn the parents that there will be noise — the sound of children enjoying themselves.

Make a real effort to get everybody to join in playing. Most children are not shy, but there may be one or two who are at your party. They will need your special help. Perhaps you can have a club member take the job of sitting with those children just to watch a game or two. Then the club member can suggest that they all try the next game together. It's the best way to send those kids home happy.

And there are so many games you can play! Here are a few for the party that your club gives. They are great for any occasion.

1. **Count the Candies.** You can start the fun even before these games begin with a candy-counting contest. You will need a large glass jar filled with hard, colored Christmas candies, a huge red bow, and pencil and paper.

Here's what you do: Fill a small glass jar with gaily colored Christmas candies, counting each one as you put it in. Tie the bow around it, and place the jar where everybody can see it. Put a pencil and a pad of paper next to it. As guests come in, let them study the jar and guess how many candies are inside. The guesses are written down, signed, and given to the host or hostess. At the end of the party, the whole candy jar goes to the guest whose guess came closest to the right answer. Even the counting up of the candies in front of all the kids after playing the games to see which guest guessed best is part of the entertainment.

2. **The Laughing Balloon.** This is an icebreaker that helps everybody have a good time right away, because it's so easy. Kids don't need to be fast, smart, or athletic. Just have a club member blow

up a balloon and knot it so that the air stays in. Everybody gathers around and follows one simple rule: When the balloon is in the air, everybody laughs. But when the balloon touches the floor or comes to rest anywhere else, everybody must stop laughing. Anybody caught laughing after the balloon is down is out. (Once you start laughing, it isn't easy to stop.) A prize can be given to the last laugher.

3. **Newspaper Relay.** Kids at a party love competition, so try this one. Divide the players into two teams. Give each team two newspapers folded into quarters. The first players from each team stand behind the starting line. At a signal from you, they race across the room and back. They race, but they don't run. This is not the Olympics. It's a house party so we have a different way to get them there and back.

Each racer must place one newspaper on the floor and step on it with one foot. Then the other newspaper must be placed for the other foot. For the third step, the first newspaper must be moved forward. *Sliding* the papers is not allowed. Each paper must be picked up for each step. When the first player gets back to the goal line, the second player on that team may start out. The first team to finish the relay with all players, wins.

4. **Flying Saucer.** All you need for this game is a wire hanger, some string, and some small paper plates. Pull down the straight bottom rung of the hanger until it forms a rough circle with a hook on top. Tie a piece of string to the hook and hang the hanger in a doorway with some cellophane tape. Players stand a few feet from the target and try to skim the paper plate "saucers" through the hanger. If you hold the plate flat and skim it, it can be aimed. Give five points for each saucer through the ring. Give the winners a small prize. You might like to give small toy airplanes as reminders of their great flying skill.

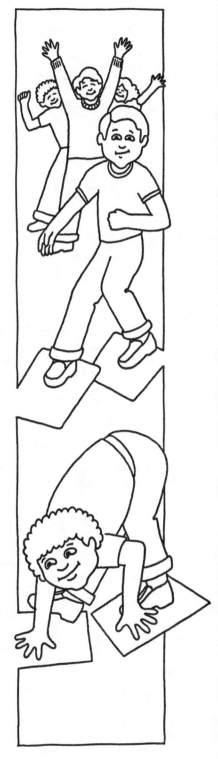

5. **Candy Cups.** This is a game you can really sink your teeth into. Each player begins with six paper cups and five wrapped candies. (If you don't have enough candies, use buttons.) Place five of the cups on a table and put one candy into each. Place the sixth cup about eight or ten inches away. Now pick up one of the paper cups between your teeth and tip it so that the candy drops into the empty cup. Do this with each of the remaining four cups. Now pile the paper cups (again with your teeth) into each other, with the cup containing all the candies on top. If you have two people playing at one time, the one who finishes first is the winner.

6. **Kitchen-Table Billiards.** This game is played with bottle tops, buttons, marbles, or poker chips. You'll need eight paper cups. Tape two cups to each

side of a kitchen or bridge table. Give each child his own "men"—bottle tops for one, buttons for another, and so on. The object is to flick the men into the side cups, using the index finger and thumb. The children take turns shooting and the first one to get his or her "men" pocketed is the winner.

7. **Breathless.** This is the kind of game that takes your breath away. Put out four ping-pong balls, two plates, and drinking straws for each player. Place the balls on one plate, and put the other plate near it. The players put straws in their mouths and suck up the ping-pong balls one by one and put them on the other plate. You can put the plates further apart if you want to make it tougher. Make sure you have spare straws on hand.

8. **Bowling Boys and Girls.** This hilarious game works best at boy-girl parties. Line up all the boys at one end of the room and have them stand on one foot. They can keep switching from foot to foot, but there must be only one foot on the ground at all times. Each girl, standing on the other side of the room, gets a chance to roll a large ball toward these human bowling pins. As the ball rolls toward the boys, they'll get jumpy. After all, standing on one leg doesn't exactly give you a sense of security. Almost always, with each roll of the ball, a few of the boys will either forget and put their feet down or lose their balance. Those boys are out. The one who remains standing on one leg the longest wins the game. Now, give the boys a chance to bowl the girls over.

9. **Shoe Scramble.** A party without girls (yes, there *are* small boys who don't know what they're missing) can get a bit noisy. One good fast game will save a lot of wear and tear on the host. Since you can't change the fact that boys are lively, let them put their high spirits into a safe scramble. Have all the kids remove their shoes and put them in the center of the room. Be sure the shoes are unlaced. Then scramble the shoes and mix them up

completely. At a signal the boys run to the shoe pile, find their own shoes, put them on, and tie the laces into a perfect bow. The first five who present themselves for inspection with neatly laced shoes are the winners. Now if some are wearing loafers or moccasins with no shoelaces, they can be the judges.

10. **Flat Head.** Has anyone ever told you, "You're not using your head?" In this game, there's no other way to play. Put three paper plates on the floor at each end of the room. Starting at one end of the room, the players pick up a plate and balance it on their heads. They then go to the other end, pick up another plate, and balance that on top of the first one. If the plates fall off (and they will), they have to start again. The first player to pick up the last plate and return to the opposite end of the room is the flat-headed winner.

11. **Paper Plates/Paper Cup Pile-Up.** In this game we add one more item to the balancing act. Put a stack of paper cups at one end of the room and a stack of paper plates at the other. The players pick up the first plate, run across and put a cup on top of it, then run back and put another plate on the cup, and so on. They must carry the stack in one hand only, building up the tower with the other hand. You can change the number of plates and cups to make the game easier or harder. Give the winning youngsters a prize—and a big hand because they really know how to use theirs.

12. **Paper Cup Fill.** Set a row of large paper cups at one side of the room. Use as many cups as there are players. Then put several ping-pong balls in separate groups at the other side of the room. The kids begin from that end, each holding a spoon. The object of the game is to scoop the ball into the spoon and carry it over to the cup and drop it in. The player who fills his or her cup first is the winner. Sound easy? Try it yourself first. Be sure to explain that the balls cannot be scooped up against the body or anything else in the room.

13. **Squeeze 'Em.** The aim here is to fill up a paper cup with water that you have put into a large bowl. Wait till the kids find out they have to do it using a sponge. The smaller the sponge the better, since they will have to soak, squeeze, and squirt more times this way. Put everything on a tray or newspaper because the players and area around them may get more water than the cup.

One of the ways you can sell parents on the whole "We'll-give-your-child's-party" idea is to tell them that your Kids-Only Club members will do the cleaning up after the party. Cleaning up includes taking down the decorations and helping straighten up the house. If you bring along a couple of large plastic trash bags, you'll be able to get the job done in no time at all.

All members should help with this chore, since everyone in the club will profit from the money going into the treasury.

Chapter 11
Putting on Any Kind of Show

Getting ready to put on a puppet show, a play, or a magic program is almost as much fun as doing it. To do it well though, you need to spend at least a couple of your Kids-Only Club meetings to prepare. You'll be glad you took this time when your audience at the end claps and claps, and friends and family tell you what a great job you did.

**Let 'Em
See You**

Make sure the audience is able to see the actors whether they're puppets or people. In theaters they do this by putting performers on a raised stage. You might use a club member's home that has a wide porch or front steps. If there is no raised area on which to perform, seat some of the audience on the floor in front, raise the next group by seating them on cushions on the floor, and put the last row on chairs in the back. Wherever they sit though, make sure that tall people are not put in the front rows. Most people's heads make poor windows.

**Let 'Em
Hear You**

The mistake new performers make most often is not speaking up. In fact, kids with loud playground voices sometimes can be barely heard—maybe because they're not sure of what they're going to say. Maybe they speak softly because they're shy. Most often kid actors or magicians or puppeteers just plain forget that you have to talk louder when you're doing a show for a bunch of people.

You don't have to shout, but you do have to make sure that people in the back can hear. You don't just "let" your voice out, you have to "send" it out! This is especially true if you're putting on a puppet play and hiding behind the stage so you can't be seen.

To make sure that the words are coming across clearly, put one of your Kids-Only Club members in the back of the room, hall, or yard. If you can't be heard, this friend can let someone backstage know. The backstage person (most probably the "stage manager") can secretly signal you to speak up. You can start checking on this at rehearsals.

The M.C.

One way to keep a show rolling while you're changing costumes, moving scenery, putting on and taking off puppets, or waiting for the next magic trick is to have a Master of Ceremonies. What this person (often called an M.C.) does will depend upon the kind of show you're putting on.

In some cases, the M.C. can "set the scene" by telling the audience where the action is supposed to be taking place (in a forest, on a beach, under the sea, on the moon), or when it is happening (a long time ago, once upon a time, today, or a thousand years from tomorrow).

For example, the M.C. could say that a scene is taking place in the woods. He or she can tell the audience about the big trees and the wild animals that live there. Audiences adore imagining and making believe along with performers. In this particular case it will also save you the trouble of making big trees and catching ferocious beasts. Or if you were doing a play about Noah's Ark, the M.C. would tell the audience how hard it was raining and how badly the ark was rocking.

Something else your M.C. could do is give "cast credits" by telling the audience the names of the performers and the parts they are playing. If you got help in making props, scenery, costumes, or anything else, this helper could also be publicly thanked. For instance, "The dishes in the show came from Mrs. Ritz's kitchen."

For a magic show the M.C. might introduce each performer and have ready some jokes, riddles, and funny announcements to tell between the tricks. Your M.C. is the one who can keep your audience happy. Pick somebody who is a good talker but who also knows when to shut up.

The Producer

Every show needs one person in charge. This should be a club member who is not in the show. As the producer, he or she watches what is going on and makes suggestions. The producer also makes sure that everything (props, puppets, costumes) is ready for the show. His or her job is to keep things moving smoothly. Most importantly, if there is a disagreement, the producer is the one who has the last word.

One performance is fun but usually not enough. Since your club gave a lot of time and effort and thought to putting together your play, puppet show, or magical program, you'll want to do it more than once. After all, there are a lot of other people around who like to be entertained.

If you're planning a performance, you might present your show first at the local nursery school for the parents, sisters, and brothers of the Kids-Only Club members, for the kids in the neighborhood, or for the local Scout troop.

This not only gives you practice, but also gives you a chance to find out from the way the audience reacts what works and what can be made better. Don't expect your show to be perfect the first time, or even the second. Just do as you practiced, then get together as a group, with the producer leading the discussion, and try to figure out what can be done better the next time.

Besides all the fun there is in being a part of all this, sometimes your show can even be a moneymaker for your club. If you plan to sell tickets, 10¢ or 25¢ for children and 50¢ for adults might be about right. You might also think about selling refreshments. A paper cup of fruit juice or lemonade would be very nice before or after the performance. And if your show has two parts, refreshments would be especially welcome during the intermission between the acts.

And now, on with the shows.

The Performance

Selling Your Show

Chapter 12
Staging a Play

A play is a great club project because you have enough people to make it a success. Besides, most people like the chance to be someone else once in a while.

If your Kids-Only Club votes on a play as its next project, here are the things to think about:

1. Picking a script
2. Deciding who is going to do what job
3. Selecting the actors and actresses
4. Finding a stage
5. Making your play come to life
6. Getting ready
7. Enjoying the big day

Picking a Script

Generally, a play works best when everything to be said on the stage is written down. There are people who have already done this, so if you try your local library, you should find many books with scripts in them that you might like. Your librarian should be very helpful here. Teachers, particularly English teachers, also have good suggestions.

Club plays are usually picked by members who make up the Play Selection Committee. This committee meets as often as needed. Each committee member reads the different plays, discusses them, and finally votes on the one the club is going to do.

The number of members in your club will help you decide which play you finally pick. You can't do a play with seven dwarfs if there are only five people in your club, while a play with three characters would not be a good choice for a club with 12 or 15 kids.

No matter what play you do, keep these things in mind:

1. A funny play is probably better for your club than a serious one. It's easier for beginning actors to make an audience laugh than to make them cry. Besides, audiences would *rather* laugh.

2. A play that has enough parts for everybody who wants to be in it will not only make your club members happy but give you a bigger audience, since parents and friends don't want to miss seeing the kids they know in action.

A Write-It-Yourself Play. Why not write an original play for your club to put on? You could "improvise" (make up) the scenes of the play with the help of other members.

Let's say you have an idea. Something happened in your life or to somebody that you know or there is a scene that you like from a book or movie. Act out your idea with other club members who also like to make believe. Keep in mind that a good scene in a play has a little "conflict." That doesn't mean a battle, with fighting and yelling. Conflict comes about when somebody wants something and can't have it. If one character wants something to happen but nobody else wants it to happen, and some people even try to keep it from happening, you'll have a lively play.

When you make up a play on your own, write it down after you have decided what everybody is going to say and do. This will be the script you need for the actors to learn their parts and for the prop and costume people to know what they need to do.

The next step is to pick the people who will be in charge of putting on the play. Some club members may have more than one job. Just make sure they don't have to do them both at the same time. You can be both an actor and a prop person, because one job is done before the play and the other job while the play is still going on. But you can't, for

Deciding Who Is Going to Do What Job

77

instance, change scenery at the same time that you have to change your costume for the next act.

Here are the jobs. If your play is simple, you may not need some of them at all.

Producer. The producer is in charge of everything, in other words, the boss of the whole play.

Director. The director helps the actors learn their lines and how to say them right. He or she runs rehearsals and works with the actors to find the best way the play should be done.

Stage Manager. Before the play, the stage manager works with the prop, scenery, costume, and makeup people to see that everything is being done. Once the play starts, he or she works back-stage to see that the play runs smoothly, making sure that everybody has the props and costumes, and also that the scenery, if you have any, is where it should be when you need it.

Prop Person. While rehearsals are going on, the prop person checks the script to collect things that are going to be needed on stage by the actors, such as a book, a mirror, a pillow, or anything else called for. Somebody who is good at details and making lists would be right for this job.

Scenery Designer. Even a one-set play can look more professional if you have one or two pieces of scenery. This might be a good job for the best artist in your group. Don't get carried away. Keep it simple, because the simplest scenery will satisfy the audience. Even a paper fence across the back of your stage can make it look like a pasture. And if they hear a "moo" or two, there will be no mistake about where they are.

Makeup Artist. Actors use makeup to make them look better or to change the way they look on stage. The person who is in charge of doing the makeup might ask one of the club mothers to show him or her how lipstick and eye shadow are used. There are books in the library on makeup. Or you might try calling your local television station and ask if you can come in to meet with their makeup person for 15 minutes or more to get tips on the best makeup for the characters in your play. And if you have moustaches, wigs, eyeglasses, and funny noses, you can change Snow White to the wicked witch in seconds, and even Prince Charming into old Rip Van Winkle.

Publicity. Even if you haven't picked your actors or actresses yet, if you want an audience someone must start telling people that your club is going to put on a play. This publicity person or committee should start well ahead of the Big Day. For hints about this very important job, see "Letting the World Know!"

Ticket Takers and Ushers. You will need a number of club members for various jobs, like selling or collecting tickets and seating the audience. They could also be the people who sell refreshments if you are going to have them. Paper cups will save you a lot of wash-up.

The actors for the different parts can be picked by the club members. Anyone who wishes to be in the club play reads for the part he or she wants. Everybody's a ham these days, so everybody may try. When all have done the reading, the club members vote and decide who gets which role. Don't think that the biggest kid always makes the best king or pirate. Sometimes the quietest kid becomes the fiercest one on stage, so give all members a crack at any part they want.

Selecting the Actors and Actresses

Where will the play be put on? A real stage with a curtain and spotlights and orchestra is nice, but not at all necessary. A front porch, a back porch, the living room or den, a classroom at school, a backyard — all of these will work as a "stage." So will an open garage (with the audience out front in the driveway), or in a driveway (with the audience in the garage).

Finding a Stage

A play can also be put on "in the round." Actors act in the center of a room or a backyard, and the audience sits all around them on cushions or chairs.

If you do your play in the round, don't use any solid props (like big cardboard cartons) that might block the audience's view. Actors who work in the round face one part of the audience for one scene and then play the next scene facing in another direction.

Making Your Play Come to Life

Costumes. If your play takes place in the past or a future time or in another country where people dress differently, you might want to put your actors in costumes, so that they will look like the characters they are playing. You don't need to get fancy. Often, just a hat will do. A cowboy or a queen, a wizard or a fireman, can immediately be identified by what they wear on their heads.

A single piece of clothing can show what a person does for a living. A white shirt put on backwards can turn you into a doctor, a bathrobe and a bandage into a patient. One piece of clothing

shouldn't be too hard to make or borrow. Neither are large paper bags. Decorating a really big one is a lot of fun and can turn you into anybody you want to be.

Scenery. Scenery is a "costume" for the stage and can make a big difference in how your play goes over. Some scenery can be just a big "prop," like a picnic table or a rocking chair. These are usually easy to get or borrow. However, if you want a tree or ocean wave or a tiger on stage, you're going to have make them yourself. The best way to do this is cut out an outline of the item you want from a cardboard carton. Then paint the carton to represent the item. If it's something like a tree, prop it with a slot of wood so it won't fall over in the middle of a performance when someone might just have finished saying, "This place is so peaceful."

Making the scenery and moving it on and off stage can be as much fun as anything else that you do because when you and your club members put your imaginations to work, anything can happen.

Sound Effects. Some plays call for certain sounds or music. You might plan some special ones for your own play. Music can come from a phonograph with a "sound person" working the machine according to the script. If certain special sounds are needed (a shout, a bell, a car motor, a scream, dishes breaking, or cars crashing), you can record them ahead of time on a tape recorder (either actually doing the action or getting it—like a car crash—from a TV program). Then the sound person can play it at the right moment in your play.

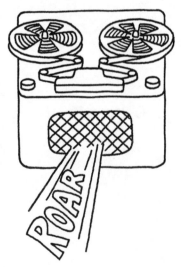

Mask Plays. An unusual presentation would be to do a play in which all the characters wear masks. You don't have to wait for Halloween either. Animal, storybook, and holiday characters (like a witch, a tin woodsman, or a Santa Claus) are easy to create in mask form and exciting to watch. Masks can be made out of paper plates, cardboard cartons, shoe boxes, ice cream tubs, paper bags.

For a paper bag mask, just make sure eyes are cut in the proper spot so actors can see through the eye holes. Then paste feathers, bits of paper, tiny paper cups, or any other material onto the bag. Don't forget the surprise touches. A party blower (one of those paper whistles that starts all rolled up and straightens out with a funny noise when you blow through it) is a lot of fun for the tongue of a paper bag character.

As for a shoe box mask, you don't wear it over the feet or over the head. A shoe box mask goes in front of the face and attaches to your ears with rubber bands.

Getting Ready

On the first day of rehearsal, the director seats all the actors in a circle, and they read from the script. Good and loud. As the reading goes on, the director can ask everybody to stand and actually do any action called for in the scene: fight the dragon, reach for the butter, or answer the phone. The director might suggest that an actor stand in a particular place and that another actor sit down when somebody speaks to him.

The actors should memorize their lines as soon as they can. When you can say your lines without looking at the script, you can begin to look at each other and make believe you are seeing Christopher Columbus, Winnie the Pooh, or Robin Hood, rather than just your own close pal.

The director will decide how many rehearsals will be needed to make the play as good as it can be. Even professional directors find that other people sometimes think of things that make the show better, so your director should listen to suggestions from the cast and crew.

While the rehearsing, stage work, and prop collecting is going on, the producer should know how members are doing at their jobs. If they need help, it's the producer who helps them or sees that they get the help they need.

Dress Rehearsal. This is the last rehearsal before the Big Day. By this time, everything should be really ready. The actors wear their costumes and use makeup, just as if the show were going to be done for a live audience. The producer, the director, and any members of the stage crew who aren't working sit on the chairs or cushions and pretend to be a regular audience. All the kinks are worked out at this time.

After this final rehearsal, the show is ready.

Enjoying the Big Day

Finally, your opening day arrives. The director has finished his work, and the stage manager takes over to get the play "on the boards." If everybody has done his job well, the props are ready, the actors are ready, and the play begins.

Of course, there'll be some goofs here or there. Professionals goof too. Someone might forget a line or drop a prop. But the whole idea is to have fun, enjoy yourself, and entertain the audience.

Best of all, you'll find that you're having the time of your life. But as much fun as you are having, you'll know that the greatest fun of all was the work you did with other Kids-Only Club members to put this play of yours together. Bravo!

Chapter 13
Doing a Puppet Show

It's as much fun to make a puppet as it is to play with one. And maybe just playing around with puppets is what you and your club friends want to do.

But if you decide that you'd like to put on a puppet play, you might make a little money for the Kids-Only Club treasury by charging admission.

Your puppets can be silly little puppets made out of almost any scrap you have around or you can create very lifelike people or animal puppets.

Here are some things you need to know if you want to put on your first puppet show:

1. How to make a puppet
2. How to work a puppet
3. How to make a stage
4. How to put on a puppet play

Any doll-like toy that moves can be called a puppet, but most puppets are either marionettes or hand puppets. Marionettes work with strings. Hand puppets move because your hand is inside, usually with your pointer finger in the neck and head, your thumb is one arm and your middle finger is the other arm.

Hand puppets are the greatest fun because they come to life so quickly. Just put one on, and he or she is ready to work for you. It (you) can do anything. If your little puppet is puzzled about something, just rub your thumb against the side of your pointing finger and watch him scratch his head. If he is happy, bring your thumb and middle finger together, and he'll clap his hands. If he is hungry you can make him rub his tummy, or if he is frightened you can make him cover his eyes.

Here's a family of hand puppets that'll be fun to have at your fingertips:

Puppet Heads. Paper cups make fine heads for puppets. Because of the wax finish and decoration on most paper cups, you may find it hard to draw on them, so make a "sleeve" of white paper to fit over the outside. To make the sleeve, take a cup and cut out the bottom. Cut down the seam and lay the cup out flat on a piece of paper. Trace around the edge to make a pattern. You can make many patterns from a single cup in this fashion. Then draw lots of different faces on the pattern until you find the one that you like.

Since glue doesn't stick very well on a paper cup either, use a paper pattern when you want to stick things onto your cup head. Paste a nose of folded paper in the right spot, or cut a little nose flap (leave the top part attached to the cup) and

How to Make a Puppet

85

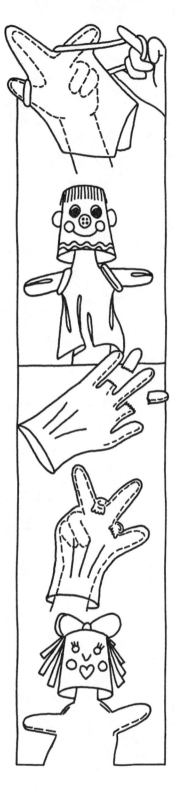

lift the flap out away from the cup. The face can be made extra funny if you paste on an extra long Pinocchio nose or your friend might like a real "button" nose.

You can make a fine head out of rubber balls that have lost their bounce or anything else that you can stick on to your pointer finger—an empty eggshell, potato, etc.

If you really want to get a head, or two, or three, collect the empty rolls from bathroom paper. Two or even three puppets can be made from each roll. Cut the rolls in halves, thirds, or quarters, depending on the length of your fingers. Paste paper around each roll or paint it. Add features by drawing or coloring with crayons or paint. The roll sits right on your pointer finger.

Since you don't want every puppet to look like Humpty Dumpty, paste hair right onto the paper cup, ball, or bathroom roll puppet. Use fringed paper, bits of fur, yarn, cloth, wool, or string, and tape it down a little on each side.

Puppet Bodies. For a drape body, fold the last two fingers of your hand into your palm and extend the other three. Drape a handkerchief over the extended fingers. Now hook a rubber band over the handkerchief around your middle finger. Pull the rubber band behind your pointer finger, and hook it around your thumb. Stick your puppet head onto your pointer finger, and you and your pal are ready to go.

The next time you lose one glove, treasure the other. It'll make a super structure for a new puppet. Cut off the ring finger and the pointer finger of the glove, leaving just enough fabric to tuck in. (If you are a righty, work with a left glove, or vice versa.) Your right thumb goes into the thumb of the glove. Your pointer finger goes into the middle finger of the glove, and your little finger goes into the pinky of the glove.

Finger Puppets. Here's a pair of puppets that may run away with your show, because instead of moving hands they have moving *feet*.

Finger Funnies—Fold a piece of cardboard that is 4 inches by 6 inches, twice, one at 1 inch from the bottom edge and again 1¾ inch from the bottom edge. Cut two holes in the first fold.

Cut out your favorite funny papers character or draw one of your own. Paste it on the cardboard. Notice that the character ends just above the knees. Cut around the character.

Now insert your first two fingers through the two holes in the fold. You can make your puppet walk and, if you have talented fingers, your puppet may even dance.

Cuppets—Just take an ordinary paper cup, and draw a face and folded arms. Then cut or poke two finger holes in the lower front. Remove the bottom of the cup. Put your fingers through the holes and, wonder of wonders, your puppet has legs.

A Paper Plate Marionette. If you'd like to have your little world on a string, here's an easy marionette to begin with. You'll need two small paper plates, four large paper plates, and some other bits and pieces.

Put the two small paper plates together face-to-face (bottoms out). Tie them rim to rim through a hole at the top. Punch another hole through the rims at the bottom.

Now put two of the large paper plates together in the same way (bottoms on the outside), and punch a hole through the top. Tie the smaller plates to the larger plates through the holes you have punched, leaving about a half-inch of string between.

The arms and legs of your marionette are made by trimming the rims from the other two large paper plates. Fasten them to the large paper plates with paper fasteners. If you twist the fasteners in their holes, it will enlarge the holes so that the

arms and legs can move freely. Tie long strings to the top of the head and to both arms and both legs. Then attach them loosely to a ruler. When you move the ruler, you move the marionette and it will walk or strut, do a waltz or a funny dance, and even wave or salute.

How to Work a Puppet

How to Make a Stage

In this case, there are no rules. No "First you do this, then you do that." Sit in front of a mirror for a few minutes with your puppet on your hand or at the end of a string and play with it. Watch it carefully. The truth is your puppet will soon be showing you how best to make it come to life.

Just one thought. It is easier to work with one puppet at a time until you've had a little practice, and your puppet tells you it wants company.

Stages are not hard to make. Most of them are already in your house. All you do is switch positions a bit. For instance, you can make a stage from an overturned chair (work from behind) or from a table turned on its side (you are on one side, the audience on the other, and the puppets on the top edge). You can work from behind an armchair with the puppets doing their act on top or over the arm.

Here are some other stages you can make.

A Tray Stage. You'll need the shallow top cover of a cardboard box, some paint, and a ribbon or a piece of heavy string. Just cut two holes large enough for your hands to fit through the box. Then paint your "stage" a bright color. Finally, attach the ribbon or string to the four corners, so that the box top will hang from your neck level with the floor. Put your hands up through the holes. Put the puppets on your hands, and let them go to work. You can even walk around with this traveling stage—to have fun wherever you go.

A Doorway Stage. Put a small table in the doorway and cover its legs with a pretty cloth. Then

TRAY STAGE

TWO CHAIRS AND A BOARD STAGE

WINDOW STAGE

DOORWAY STAGE

raise your hands, covered with puppets, up to the edge of the tabletop. If you don't have a table, just tack a cloth across the doorway and raise your hands above the cloth—with your puppets on, of course.

Tack or tape some scenery to the wall in back of the doorway, or to some cardboard boxes placed a few feet in back of the doorway. Then put your puppets between the scenery and the audience for a wonderful effect.

A Window Stage. If you have a main floor window, stand or sit on the outside with only your puppets showing through the window. The audience can sit in the room. Or turn the whole idea around. That is, work your puppets from inside the room while the audience sits in the yard outside. You have an extra piece of equipment this way. Though it was never meant to be used as such, the window shade would make a fine curtain for your show.

Two Chairs and a Board. Place two chairs apart and lay a board between them. Now drape a pretty cloth (a tablecloth, a bedspread) over the board so that it reaches the floor.

A Big Stage. You can construct bigger puppet stages from large cardboard boxes, or from a number of small ones mounted together.

How to Put on a Puppet Play

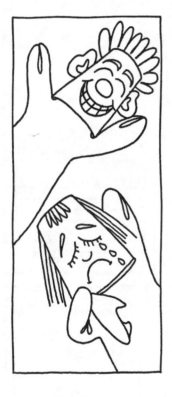

Here's something about puppets that is a little known secret. If a puppet in a play is sad, it is seldom just a little sad. It is very, *very* sad. Puppets are not just happy, they are very, *very* happy. A bad puppet is very bad, and a good puppet is very good.

No matter what your play is, the first puppet actor on stage in your show should begin with a bang! Either have your puppet almost fly onto the stage to surprise your audience or let it peek out from behind the curtain to get their attention.

Whatever you do, get your puppet show started with action. Although puppets can do all kinds of things on stage, the thing they do best is make an audience laugh. A hand puppet might come on with a blown-up balloon, aim it at the audience, and let go of it. The balloon will zig and zag all around before some lucky member of the audience catches it. Of course, you are the one holding the unknotted balloon between your thumb and your middle finger, aiming it, and then letting go of the balloon.

Like everybody else, puppets like to get around in style. They don't just have to walk on and off the stage. Give them a little fancy transportation. Let them ride on motor bikes, planes, trains, sailing ships, horses, or rockets. Use your own lightweight toys. If you'll stick them on a ruler or a long pencil with paste or tape, you can work them on the stage. You can even use magazine cutouts of these things, pasted onto cardboard, and attached to a long stick.

Whatever puppet play you decide to put on, you will want to keep things as easy and simple as possible.

1. Remember that two or three puppeteers can work at the same time to give you group scenes and lots of action. It also gives more club members a chance to perform.

2. Different kinds of puppets work nicely with one another. A paper cup puppet will work with a ball puppet, and they won't fight unless you want them to. Real people also work well with your puppet characters. You may wish to consider a puppet M.C. who would have his own little stage from which he sets a scene, comments on the action, or even talks to the audience while the other performers are changing the scenery or putting on and taking off puppets.

3. Try to keep the show to only one or two settings so that you don't have to change scenery too often.

4. All the ideas mentioned in the "Staging a Play" chapter for making a play come to life can also be used for a puppet play.

Which Play? There are many good library books with plays for puppets. Best of all, your club could write its own play. In the chapter on "Staging a Play," you'll find information on choosing your own story. The hints in the play chapter work just as well for puppet shows.

Without a doubt, a puppet show is fun to watch. But it is even more fun if you and your club members have a hand in the action.

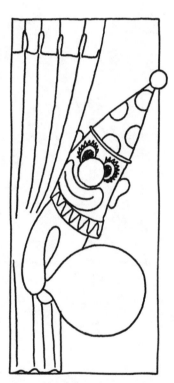

Chapter 14
Making Magic

It's always hard to tell who's having the most fun at a magic show: the audience or the magician.

You have no magician in the club? Well, being a nonmagician is only a temporary problem. It can be corrected just by reading this chapter.

There are several good reasons why your Kids-Only Club might put on a magic show:

1. Just for the sheer fun of magic
2. To raise money
3. To practice doing magic as part of your party-throwing business (see Chapter 10)
4. So that everybody in the club can learn magic to do at the dinner table with spoons and forks, or at school during lunch hour with paper cups, or out in the playground using pennies and nickles, or anywhere.

Magic is not just for kids. The fact is, everybody is a kid where magic is concerned. But you can't tell *everybody* about your trick because magic is all about secrets. How the trick works is your secret. If you're going to be a good magician, you must be good at keeping the secret, so practice in private (or with your Kids-Only Club friends) until nobody can see how you're doing what you're doing. Remember, there's one strict rule about magic: magicians *never* tell.

Do a Magic Trick

There are four things that will help you do your trick well and earn you the name "Magician."

1. Preparation
2. Surprise
3. Misdirection
4. Presentation

Preparation. Some tricks appear to be done right "on the spot" with "no getting ready" at all. But most magic tricks really do require a little bit of advance work. You might have to hide a coin or fold a paper in a certain way or even work out a trick with somebody who will be in the audience. As you go on to the tricks in this book, you will see that most of them require some preparation.

Surprise. Surprise your audience with your tricks by doing them, not by telling them what you are going to do.

A good trick is like a good joke; it should take you by surprise. If people know where to watch for the coin to appear, it won't be as much fun.

Also, it is possible that the trick might go a little wrong. If that happens, you may still be able to do something to cover the mistake, but you can't make it work if you have already told your audience just what is supposed to happen, and then it doesn't.

Misdirection. Almost every trick needs this magic secret. All it means is that you cause your audience to look or think *here,* while you are doing something *there*. You will get them to watch *one* hand, while you are doing something with the *other* hand. You will understand this better after you read the tricks in this book.

Presentation. A magician doesn't have to be a tall, dark, bearded man with a long, black cape. A good magician can be anyone. You. Just be yourself, keep your show simple, and you'll surprise them all.

Putting on Your Magic Show

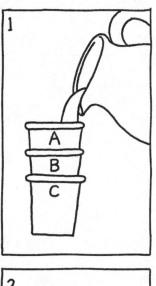

You can have three or four or five or six or even ten magicians performing in your program. By taking turns, with each magician doing no more than two tricks at a time, your audience will stay alert as each new performer comes on stage.

Even if you have a stage manager who is helping everyone, each magician should be responsible for his own tricks. This is the best way to make sure that every prop is where you want it, when you want it.

It's better to practice a few tricks and have them down very well than to do a lot of tricks and goof some of them. So for your show, concentrate on those tricks that you do best rather than the ones that you are just learning.

Don't worry about somebody in the audience jumping up and yelling, "Hey, I know how you did that." Most audiences are too polite to let people in on the secret even if they know it or think they know it. If you do get a heckler from the audience who shouts, "I know how you did that," just say, "Isn't that amazing. I know how I did that too," and go on with your stunts.

The following tricks are good ones to start with. There are books and books in your public library which will teach you many more.

Dry Water. Start by carefully cutting out the flat bottom of a paper cup. Then place three paper cups into one another with the bottomless one (Cup B) in the middle.

Pour water from a pitcher into your top cup (Cup A, see Figure 1). Then lift it off the stack and place it on your table (see Figure 2). Ask the audience which cup contains the water. When they say Cup A, you can quickly agree, but ask them to keep their eyes on where the water goes.

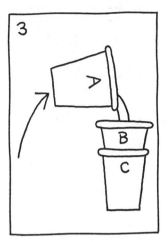

Pick up Cup A and pour the water from it into Cup B (which doesn't have a bottom, see Figure 3.) Next, carefully lift Cup B and put it down on the table on the other side of Cup C (see Figure 4). Everybody will think that Cup B has water in it, but because you have secretly removed the bottom, the water has gone through into Cup C. Now ask your audience again where the water is, and when they point to Cup B, tell them, "Oh, no, you weren't watching." Pick up Cup B, holding it so that your hand covers the hole in the bottom, and turn it upside down. Then put it carefully on the table. Pick up Cup C, and pour the water from it into Cup A. The water will appear to have vanished from Cup B and somehow "traveled" into Cup C.

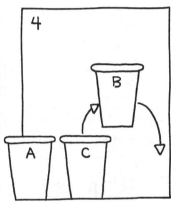

Casually pile your cups back into one another, nesting them as before with the bottomless cup in the middle and the filled cup on the top.

Double Your Money. All you need for this trick is two one-dollar bills and a shirt with a collar. One dollar bill should be crumpled into a ball and secretly wedged between your collar and the back of your neck (Figure 1). The second dollar bill starts out in your wallet.

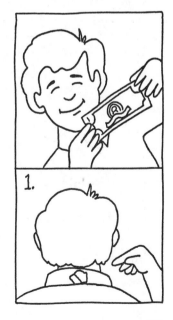

Remove the dollar from the wallet, and show everyone that it's a single bill. If they don't believe you let them handle the money. Crumple it into a round ball and hold it between the very tips of your left fingers and thumb. Then tell your audience that in order to do the trick with the bill, you have to rub it on your elbow for luck.

Bend your arm, and as you rub the bill on your right elbow, the fingers of your right hand should

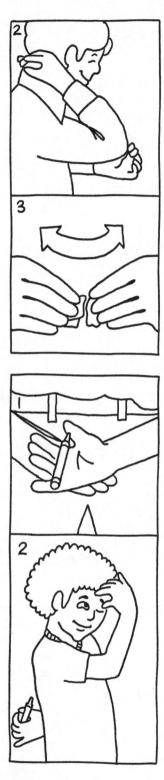

secretly take the bill that you've hidden behind your collar (Figure 2). When you have that bill in your fingers (which are still at your collar), stop rubbing the first bill and look at it closely. Explain that it looks like you didn't rub it enough, and as you lower your right arm, take the bill you've been rubbing into your right hand, and add it to the secret bill that you took from behind your collar.

Now double up your left arm as if you were making a muscle. Rub your left elbow with the two bills that are held in your right hand, telling your audience that your right elbow doesn't seem to contain its usual magic. At this point, bring your two hands together, transfer one of the bills from your right hand to your left hand. Then pull your hands apart as though you were tearing a bill in half (Figure 3). Roll each of the bills in your fingers for a second or two and then drop them separately on the table.

Magic Crayon. A box of crayons and a fingernail are all you need for this one.

Give an unopened box of crayons to someone in the audience. Turn your back while that person selects one and shows it to everyone else. With your back still to the audience and your hands behind your back, have someone put the crayon into your hands so that you can't see it (Figure 1).

Turn around to face your audience and ask them to think very hard of the color selected. As they are concentrating, with the little finger of the hand not holding the crayon, scrape a bit of the crayon coloring onto your fingernail. Then, as you concentrate, bring the marked hand out from behind your back and hold it to your forehead (Figure 2), making sure that the audience can see that it is definitely empty. Think for a moment with your eyes closed, and tell the audience you are getting their message. Open your eyes, and as you take your hand away from your forehead, glance at your finger and tell them the name of the color.

String Thing. You will need a piece of thick white string, the kind made up of eight or twelve smaller strands twisted into one large strand. Cut a length about 18-inches long, and in the center separate the small strands into two equal parts for about three inches (Figure 1). Let the two sections retwist themselves, and you'll have a piece of string with two "horns" on it. Glue the two real ends of the string together with a little bit of white glue (Figure 2). Now you're ready for your trick.

Hold the strings between your thumb and finger where the "horns" meet the string. It looks as though you're holding a regular length of string near the two ends. Put the first finger and thumb of the other hand on the dab of glue, and pull the loop of the string tight so that the two strands can be cut just above the glue (Figure 3).

Now have your helper cut the strands just above the glue. Then hold the string by the two new ends that your friend has just made. Put the "horns" inside your fist, and ask your helper to gently pull on his other ends. Rub the center of the string inside your fist and when you open your fist, the "horns" will have retwisted themselves into a whole string (Figure 4).

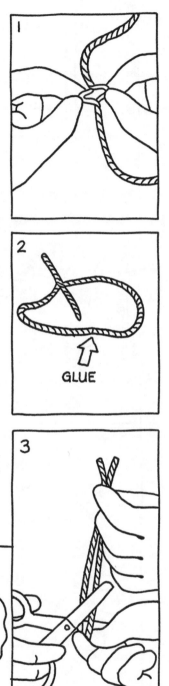

GLUE

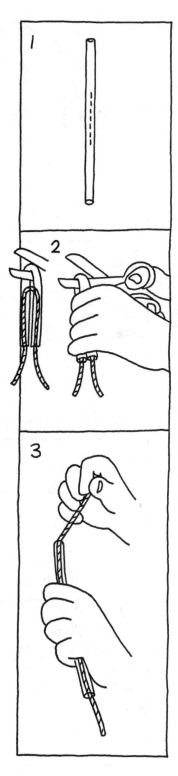

1

2

3

Cut and Uncut. With this trick you will show your audience that you can thread a string through a straw, double the straw over, cut it in half, but that when the string is pulled out it will not have been cut.

Ahead of time very carefully cut a two-inch slit in the center of the straw (Figure 1). Throughout the trick, handle the straw by the ends so the slit stays closed and unnoticed.

When you're ready to do the trick in front of your audience, push very thin kite or package string through the straw until it's hanging out of each end. Bend the straw in half so the slit is on the inside of the fold. Grip the straw in your left fist and pull the two ends of the string with your right hand. This will pull the string out of the center of the straw and through the slit so that it is an inch below the fold.

Pick up a scissor and put the lower blade through the fold of the straw, but above the string, and cut (Figure 2). Take the lower end of the straw in your right fingers, and pull the string and the straw down into your left fist until they stick out the bottom. Lift one end up all the way between your thumb and your index finger so that you now have an end of straw sticking out of your left fist (Figure 3). Wave the scissors over your left hand, and pull out the string to show that it has been restored.

Stolen Treasure. For this one you need a handkerchief, a small object from the pocket of a member of the audience, and one of your Kids-Only Club members to act as your secret helper.

Borrow a handkerchief and ask somebody to give you a small object, perhaps a ring. Hold the object in your right fingers and cover with the handkerchief (Figure 1). Now offer the covered hand to somebody in the audience so he or she can reach under and feel the object resting safely in your fingers. Have two or three people check to make

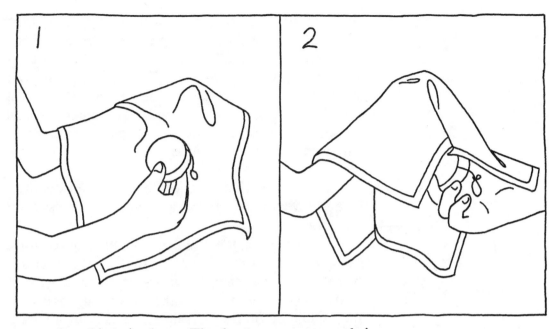

sure the object is there. The last person to reach in and feel the object should be your helper. Your friend removes the object from between your fingers while you make sure that the fingers stay in the same position so that the handkerchief keeps its shape (Figure 2). Now snap your fingers. Taking a corner of the hanky in your left hand, shake out the empty cloth and return it to its owner. When the person who gave you the ring asks for it back, tell him you'll give it to him at the end of the performance and then secretly get it back from your confederate.

That's It! Here's another trick that requires a little help from another Kids-Only clubber. You go out of the room, and the audience selects an object in the room which you are to identify when you return. When the object has been selected, you are called back into the room and your friend starts naming or pointing to different objects, asking if that is the one picked by the group. He can name four, five, or six objects, and everybody will be watching so that he doesn't give you any signal.

The trick is that you will be signaling him. When you want him to name the selected object, you merely do something to change your position—fold or unfold your arms, shift one foot, put your hands behind you, or some other natural movement—which you and your friend have agreed on in advance. As soon as he sees you make your move, the next object he names will be the selected one.

This is the kind of trick that you can do twice because everybody will be looking at your assistant instead of you.

Three-Cup Betcha. When you start, place three paper cups in front of you so that only one cup is bottoms up, the other two bottoms down (Figure 1). It doesn't matter whether the bottom-up cup is in the middle or on the outside. Say to your audience "I'll bet you can't turn over two cups at a time, and in three moves end with all three cups bottoms up." (As you talk, turn over the cups, half-turn each time so that a cup that was bottoms down becomes bottoms up, and vice versa (Figure 2). By the time you have finished talking, turn the two cups that are bottoms down, bottoms up (Figure 3).

You then place the cups in front of someone else and say, "You do it." They can't. They really can't! You perform the "betcha" again, and they still can't do it!

Here's how the trick works. (Make sure no one is reading over your shoulder now. This trick is no fun if anyone else knows the secret.) When you have successfully completed demonstrating the stunt, all three cups will be bottoms up. As you put the three cups in front of someone else, casually turn one over so that two cups are bottoms up and only one is bottoms down (Figure 4). The trick can't possibly work this way. After they try (and fail), the cups ought to be set up so that you can do the trick again. If they are not, fix them so that only one cup is bottoms up. If you had your

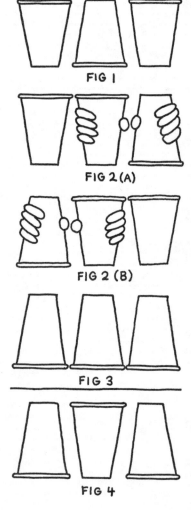

FIG 1

FIG 2 (A)

FIG 2 (B)

FIG 3

FIG 4

bottoms-up cup in the middle the first time you did the trick, put it on the outside this time,

Sometimes, by accident, someone will start the stunt with the cups in the correct position (only one cup bottoms up). When this happens, very mysteriously say, "I'm going to give you the magic touch, and the trick will work for you this time." Touch the person's forehead as you say this, and watch his surprise as he manages to do it right.

The Floating Body. Things are not always what they seem. This trick is a good example because it uses illusion (something magicians use all the time) to create a certain effect. To do the trick you will need an assistant, as well as these items: a large bed sheet, two towels, two sticks about three or four feet long, a pair of shoes and socks to match the ones your assistant is wearing.

First you'll need to prepare some fake legs. Tie one sock and one shoe at the end of each stick. To give the "leg" some shape, take the towels, roll them lengthwise, and tie one to each stick. Tie the two sticks together. Now take a long, low bench and place a cover over it that will reach the floor. This way the audience cannot see the other side where you have placed the fake legs on the floor beside you. Now you are ready to do the trick.

Have your assistant come on stage and straddle the bench, one leg on each side. Take the bed sheet and hold it between your assistant and

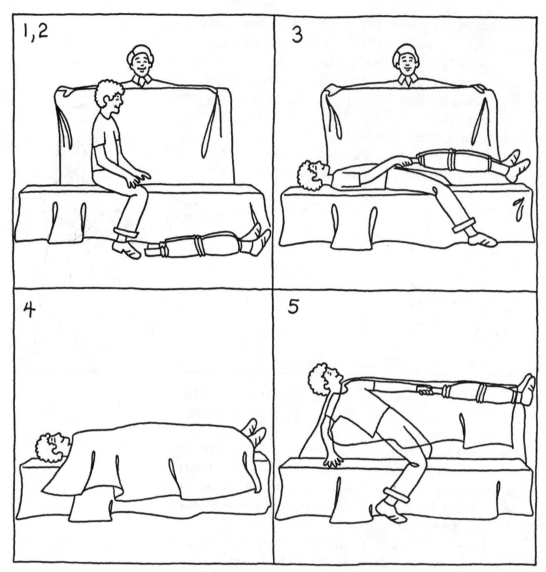

audience. Your helper takes the false legs and lies on the bench with the false legs in the position his real legs would have been in. Now cover him with the sheet so that the only things showing are his head and the fake feet. Your helper places his right hand on the bench and very slowly puts his head back and stands, holding the fake legs level with his left hand and raising them as he stands. From the audience's side, the effect is astonishing. With practice you and your helper ought to be able to work this trick so well it will fool everybody into thinking he is really floating in mid-air.

Ball Disappearance and Reappearance. For this trick, all you need is a single paper cup and a small ball made out of tin foil or paper. Cut away half of the bottom of the paper cup, and you are ready to go.

Turn the cup upside down, with the part of the bottom that is cut away towards the rear (away from the audience), and place your tin foil ball so that it rests on what remains of the bottom. The audience will not be able to tell that part of the bottom isn't there because they will see the ball resting on what remains.

To perform this trick, you reach over to get the ball so that the back of your hand blocks the audience's view of the ball. As you are closing your hand over what the audience thinks is the ball, slide the ball into the hole. At this point the ball is on the table inside the cup, and you have made a fist out of your hand. Make a throwing gesture with your closed fist, as if you were throwing the ball into the cup. Open your fist to show the audience that the ball has disappeared, and then lift up the cup showing that the ball is now underneath.

Wet and Dry. For this trick, you need a big paper cup and a small paper cup. Paste the small one inside the big one just below the rim. Wedge a crumpled napkin or tissue (colored, if possible) into the small cup, so that it will not fall out when you turn the large cup over. Turn the large cup over, so the audience sees that you have nothing in the bottom, but don't show them the inside of the cup.

Now take another cup with a little water in it. Pour some water into your large cup, making sure as you pour that it goes between the small cup and the large cup. After you have filled the bottom of the large cup, say your magic words, and reach in and pull out the dry napkin from the small cup.

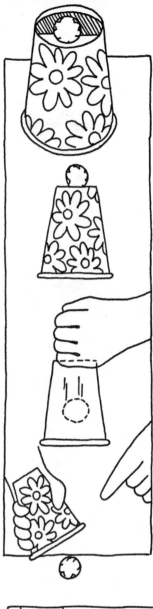

The Magic Cup. For this trick, you will need a large paper cup, a piece of cardboard, glue, a juice glass (or some other small glass), some ribbons (or streamers), rice (or beans, sand, confetti), and a "magician's" high hat (or an empty box).

Cut a circle from the cardboard slightly smaller than the circle formed by the top of the paper cup. Wedge this cardboard circle into the cup so that it forms a false bottom for your cup approximately 1 inch down from the rim. Glue it into place. Now cut the bottom out of your paper cup. Fill the small glass with your streamers and ribbons, and place the paper cup over the small glass so that the glass is hidden. You are now ready to do the trick.

Show the audience that the hat or box is empty. Hold the cup so that your little finger stops the glass from falling out. Holding the cup over the hat, put a few grains of rice (or the beans, sand, confetti) from the top part of your cup into the hat. Then tell your audience that you have put too many grains into the hat, and lower the paper cup into the bottom of the hat. At the same time, take out a few of the grains that you have previously put into the bottom of the hat and put them back into the top of the cup. This is done to distract your audience. The important thing for you is to leave the glass in the bottom of the hat as you remove the paper cup.

Now pick up your paper cup with the rice (or beans, sand, confetti) and put it aside. Say some magic words over your hat, and pull the streamers (or ribbons) one at a time out of the glass, which is safely resting in the formerly empty hat. The last object you should remove is the glass. When you do this trick, everybody will take their hats off to you.

The next two tricks make cute closers for any magic performance. They'll bring you a hand, a groan, and the pleasure of knowing you left them laughing.

The Great What-Is-It. All that's required for this trick is a large scarf, a magician in loafers (or shoes which have been previously untied), and the nerve to do it.

Walk to the front of your stage or fairly close to the audience, and point out to them that there is nothing on the floor at your feet. Make sure to get their agreement before you proceed. Then bend over, hold the scarf by the upper two corners, letting the lower two corners hang down so that they touch the floor in front of your shoes. Now, protecting your legs and feet from the audience's view with the scarf, slip your feet out of your shoes, step back one step, and pull the scarf so that it begins to drape over the shoe that you have taken off. It will seem as if something has mysteriously appeared on the floor.

When you step back further and raise the scarf revealing your empty loafers, everyone will recognize that as a magician, few people can fill your shoes.

Water Under a Hat. This is as much a joke as it is a trick. Place a paper cup of water on a table and cover it with a hat. Then tell your audience that you will drink the water without removing the hat. Then get under the table and pretend you are drinking the water. After this, invite a skeptic to remove the hat to see if the water is gone. As soon as the hat is removed, drink the water and remark that, see, you *did* drink the water without removing the hat. They removed the hat for you.

Chapter 15
Kids' Conservation Gang

Start a kids' conservation gang. You may not believe it, but kids *can* make a difference. You can do things that will really improve your corner of the world, and make it cleaner, prettier, safer, and nicer for you and all the other people and animals who share it with you.

Some of the following projects may not be just right for your area, but almost every neighborhood can use help of some kind.

Adopt a Plot

Find a spot in your neighborhood or your town where litter is a problem. This could be a beach or part of a nearby park. It might be a vacant lot. Get permission from the owners or the person who runs the park or beach to clean the area. Not for pay, but just to help nature. Set a day and ask all the Kids-Only Club members to show up for the job. Get some big trash bags and be sure everybody is wearing gloves as there might be some sharp things in the litter and this can be dangerous. Then clean up that plot. You'll be surprised how much difference a group of kids can make in a short time on a piece of littered land.

After you finish, perhaps the owner will let you put up a "Don't Litter" sign. He or she might even let you put up a sign that says, "Please help us. This area is being kept clean by (the name of your club)."

You might even plant flowers (seeds don't cost much) or shrubs to discourage littering and brighten up the area. Think about choosing flowers that can also provide food for birds. Honeysuckle, sunflower, and berry bushes are all plants on which birds and animals can feed.

You'll find that many of your neighbors (particularly elderly ones) would like to improve the way their lawns and gardens look, but don't have the time or strength to do it themselves, nor the money to hire help. Your Fix-It Team can get in there with their people power and energy. There's so much that you can do: pick up leaves, weed gardens, shovel snow, mow and water lawns. You can charge a little if the neighbors are willing and able to pay, but the important thing is to brighten up the place where you live. Once you have started, maybe others will pick up on your good idea.

Be a Fix-It Team

Get Cash for Trash

There are many things that you can collect and then sell. Not only will this help raise money for your club, but you will be doing something about conservation rather than just talking about it. Did you know that about 100 pounds of newspapers and magazines will add about $1.00 to your treasury? You can also collect and get paid for cartons of aluminum cans. Not bad for things everybody uses and conveniently piles outside their doors.

Before your club starts collecting the stuff, first find out where you can sell your collection. If there's no place to sell it within a reasonable distance, you'll be stuck with a heap of trash rather than a heap of money. Look in the Yellow Pages of the phone book under "Waste Paper" to find a salvage or junk company eager to buy. Even if the people you talk to don't want it, they may be able to give you the name of someone who will.

Next, decide how you will collect. Probably the best method is house-to-house. Some clubs slip flyers (handprinted or mimeographed sheets) under each door in the neighborhood telling which day they will make their pickup. They ask people to simply leave their tin or aluminum cans or piles of newspapers at a certain spot by the side of the house. In this way, you won't disturb anyone by ringing the doorbell.

It's very important that the collection be made on the announced day. Nothing will kill neighborhood confidence in your club faster than not following through on the plan.

Then on collection day, your club members can come with wagons, or have a volunteer parent drive a car to go door to door picking up the scrap materials and taking them directly to the collection center. Make sure the center is open on the day you plan to deliver.

In this way, you will not only increase your club's treasury, but you'll come down on litter and solid waste in your neighborhood.

We all know that cat and dog food comes in cans, but so far there's no such thing as canned bird food. City birds especially have a tough time finding food in the winter. Your club members can help birds survive by opening outdoor cafeterias.

Cup Feeder. Cut down the sides of a small paper cup so it forms a shallow container. Thread a needle, stick it through both sides of the cup, make a loop, and tie a knot. Mix a teaspoonful of peanut butter (yep, birds love the stuff, too) with an equal amount of crumbs. Put this into your little paper bucket and hang it right on the branch of a tree. Birds also like hardboiled eggs, crackers, popcorn, pumpkin seeds, and bits of cheese in their paper cup feeders. How's that for bird food!

Fat Strings. Have each club member take chunks of fat cut off meat at home and save it in the refrigerator, wrapped in waxed or aluminum foil paper until your next meeting. Then when you meet, use a needle and a length of strong thread (fishing line will do) and make a long string of these tasty lumps. Drape the string, like a Christmas tree decoration, on a branch of a tree as high as you can reach. This will keep it out of the way of cats and will give the birds fat to eat and burn when the weather turns cold. You can also scatter nuts, seeds, and crumbs on the ground for ground-feeding birds.

Bird Doughnut Shop. A doughnut is shaped so perfectly that it simplifies what you have to do. Just tie a string through the hole and let it swing from a tree branch. It will be a great free-floating treat for the birds.

For a longer-lasting doughnut feeder, you will need two jar lids, a long nail, a doughnut, and some string. Make a hole in the center of each lid with the nail. Poke the nail through the bottom lid, the doughnut, the top lid, and then tie the string firmly around the end of the nail. Hang the feeder on a branch by the string.

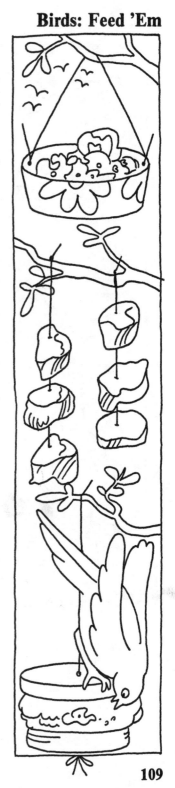

Birds: House'Em

Pine Cone Cafe. Pine cones make fantastic serving dishes for those on the wing. If you have any lying on the ground in your neighborhood, collect them. Then spread each pine cone with peanut butter, sprinkle on seeds of any kind, and hang it from a tree branch.

Feathered Folk Fruit Holder. Birds like fruit, too. Cut an apple into slices, stick a hairpin holder into it, and spear it on a small branch.

When your mother has company, she likes to prepare things she knows they will enjoy. So for birds visiting your area, you might serve their favorite foods. Mocking birds like bread crumbs, chickadees favor mixed seeds, cardinals love sunflower seeds. Most birds appreciate fat and suet (which is another kind of fat), fruits like raisins, and cut-up bits of orange and apple.

And now that they're fed up, maybe they'd like to wash and drink up.

Bird Fountain. On snowy days birds often die of thirst because the water they drink is covered by snow or sometimes turns into ice. You can help if you leave little paper cups of water, cut down, so they're shallow enough for birds to reach with their little beaks.

If you want to find out more about birds in your neighborhood and other ways you can keep them alive and chirpily happy during the winter, call your local fish and game wildlife officer. He'll give you more tips.

In city, suburb, or country, birds can use shelters during the cold winter and the rainy season. Here are some amusing ones your club can make.

Milk Carton Camper. Cut a square opening about 3½ inches high in the front and back of a milk carton. Stick a branch through as a perch from front to back so the birds have somewhere to land. Then poke a hole through the top part of the carton, pull a string through, and hang your milk carton camper on a branch. Stock cereal, bread-crumbs, or fruit in the camper for your friends.

Bleach Bottle Bungalow. Cut a hole (front and back) in a large washed plastic bleach or detergent bottle. The hole should be in the lower part of the bottle. To the bottom, glue an old aluminum pie tin or a disposable aluminum dish from a frozen food package. This will give the birds a ledge to stand on. Hang on a tree branch. Instant bird shelter.

If your club members want to do a good bird-housing job, they should know these things in order to make their home a sweet home.

Do put the birdhouse up high. If you make more than one, put them on different trees. Birds like privacy, too.

Keep the birdhouses in partial sunlight with the back of the houses to the usual wind direction.

Don't make the openings too small.

Don't put the birdhouse where cats, squirrels, weasels, or small children can get at it.

Show 'Em and Tell 'Em

There are a couple of things you can do to tell people what some other conservation problems are and explain what you think they might do about these problems.

Make Posters. Posters are a good way of telling people what you want them to know. Make conservation posters and put them around town. If your poster wants to remind people to reuse paper bags, you might suggest that they take used grocery bags back to the store when they go to shop.

Your poster might be about saving electricity, saving water, avoiding litter, and other pollution solutions. Don't worry that you are telling grownups what they already know. People forget and need to be reminded.

Write a Letter. Tell somebody if you are unhappy about the air, the water, the streets, or any other part of your environment. It's your world. You, too, have rights, and deserve to be heard.

Write a letter to the mayor of your city. Write to your congressperson. Say exactly what bothers you and tell what you think should be done. And by all means, mention what you and your Kids-Only Club members are doing to help.

Let's say you are upset about the mess in the streets. Your letter might read: "Dear Mayor, We are the 10 (or 12) members of the Kids-Only Club, and we live in your city. The streets of our neighborhood are full of litter. We think it looks awful. We need more trash cans because when we pick up papers, there is no place to put them. What can we do to make sure we get more trash cans in our neighborhood? We are looking forward to hearing your answer very soon. Thank you."

Now, have all of your club members sign it. Be sure to include your address. If you don't get an answer to this letter, write another.

If you and your friends are really interested in conservation and ways you can help, call your local Department of Fish and Game and ask them for pamphlets and bulletins on what to do to improve the environment. They'll have many ideas you may want to use. Also keep your eye out for news on television or in the paper of other conservation groups. You might want to contact them to see if you can join in some of their activities.

Find Out More

Chapter 16
Letting the World Know!

If other people know about your Kids-Only Club, you'll discover many other friends will want to join. You'll also find that if local merchants and businessmen hear about what a great group of kids you are, they will be more likely to help you by printing things cheaply for you (maybe even free), or saving scraps of wood and fabric, or putting aside big cartons for booths or puppet stages.

So one of your most important committees is the publicity committee. The head of it might be the same person for a year, or you might change with each event.

The committee's job is to tell the public about your special play, or carnival, or fair, or whatever activity you are doing.

If the public is going to be invited the publicity committee helps people make up their minds to attend and buy tickets. They do this by telling everybody what a great event your club is going to run and how small the cost is compared to the amount of fun they will have.

The committee lets the world know by word of mouth, posters, flyers (printed sheets given out in the neighborhood), by contacting local newspapers, radio, and TV stations, and by any other methods they can think of.

For the right event, you might even try having club members walking on the busiest street in town in a sandwich sign. It is bound to attract a lot of attention. For a little more razzle dazzle and if you really want to put on the dog, do put the sign on a dog. If you have a big dog that belongs to a club member, see whether it can be persuaded to wear a cardboard sandwich sign, too. If the dog cooperates, everybody will look at that message. After all, the circus, with elephants, monkeys, and bands, sometimes parades down Main Street to let everybody know of their big event, so why shouldn't you use Rover, Napoleon, or Lassie?

Word of Mouth

The best publicity in the world is word of mouth. When one person tells another, it's more convincing than anything that can be read in the newspaper or heard about on radio and television. So tell your friends about your carnival, craft fair, play, or community activity. Ask your friends to tell their friends. If possible, do it in front of a crowd—by announcing it at a school assembly or to any other group of people who might be interested in coming to your event. This is no time to be shy and sit in a corner, twiddling thumbs and hoping maybe somebody will show up. Let the world know of your Kids-Only Club activity. It will pay off. It may be just the thing your own little world is waiting to hear.

Flyers

Prepare handdrawn or typed sheets that tell about your program. Since photocopying is usually a fairly expensive way to duplicate flyers in quantity, ask your local instant printer about other methods he has for inexpensive reproduction. Maybe he will contribute paper and printing in exchange for a credit line on the bottom of your announcement, such as "This flyer was printed as a public service for the Kids-Only Club by _____."

When you are ready to distribute them, do not go around the neighborhood alone. Go in pairs and slip the flyers under doors or in mail slots. If you preplan your sheet, the top can be cut out to hang on door knobs, or you can use rubber bands or transparent tape to attach to door knobs.

To be sure that your efforts end up as a plus and not a minus for your club's image, here are three handy tips: 1) When you distribute your flyers, don't disturb people by ringing doorbells. 2) Don't open mailboxes to put things in—it's against the law. 3) Don't leave flyers lying around to mess up the neighborhood.

Posters

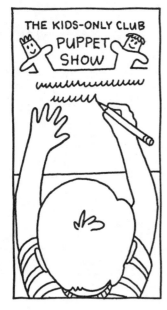

A poster uses words and pictures to tell what an event is, when it is, and where it is. It must be easy to understand at a glance and easy to read. It's like a billboard—only not as big. It's like a commercial—only it's read, not said. Posters will do a good job for you if you make them early—at least two or three weeks before your event, so that people have a chance to see them and make plans to attend.

How to Make Them. You can use any kind of paper (even ordinary typing paper), but heavyweight construction paper or cardboard is the best. It won't wrinkle easily or tear. You don't want your poster to last forever, but you do want it to last at least until your event.

Since you want to get your poster into a store window, don't make it bigger than 12 inches by

18 inches. After all, the store window is where the owner sells his own goods, and he won't want to give you more space than he has himself.

You can hand letter your poster with colored felt-tipped pens or crayons to attract attention. Some poster-makers cut letters from newspapers and magazines. Stencils work very well, too. Three-dimensional posters using bits of material, twigs, feathers, leaves, little paper cups, or paper plates, pasted onto the poster are real eyecatchers.

But the most important thing on your poster to remember is to make BIG, EASY-TO-READ letters.

How to Spread Them Around. Give a free ticket to the store owner who agrees to put a poster

in his window. This will build up an audience (especially if he brings along his wife and 10 children) and also provide goodwill for your club. If you pick up the poster from the store after the event, it will make a nice memento of your Kids-Only Club activity—and please the store owner, too.

Don't overlook the front window of club members' homes. Other good places to put up a notice are the school, church, synagogue, and community bulletin boards.

Put posters where the kinds of people that you want to come will be sure to see them. For example, if you are putting on a craft fair, you wouldn't go to a gas station. You'd go to the local craft and hobby shops, yarn shops, and others like that. If it's a backyard carnival, ask the local ice cream parlor, stationery store, or toy store to display your poster. Put your posters in places where you'll find your audience—at the local YMCA or YWCA and park recreation center.

But whatever you do, don't glue posters to fences, walls, trees, or anything. Use tape or tacks and take them down after the event is finished.

Radio, Television, and Newspapers

Sure! It's possible. Your local stations may well call your announcement "public service." They are often happy to tell about what young people are doing and may describe your event "on the air."

Smaller radio and TV stations and local newspapers are more likely to use your announcement than bigger ones. But to do it, radio, television, and newspaper people need a good "news release" telling them all about your event before they can help you let the world know about it.

Your News Release. Your news release can be neatly handwritten or printed, but most radio, TV, and newspaper people agree that they would rather get a typed release with double spaces between the lines. Perhaps you could have a parent or helpful, friendly adult lend a hand with the typing.

In the news release be sure that you:

1. Tell all the important facts of the event in the first paragraph. Tell what is happening, when, where, who is putting on the event, and why. If you're going to be charging the public, you should also tell how much.

2. Double check all names, addresses, and facts to make sure that they're right (and spelled right).

3. At the top of the page of your news release, give the name and address of the club, and both the name and phone number of the publicity chairman or the person in charge of the event. If the newsperson wants to ask any more questions, he or she then knows whom to call.

4. Include the date you would like your information to be printed or broadcast. This should also be in the first page of your news release in the upper left-hand corner. If you want your event announced as soon as it is received, put "For Immediate Release."

5. Make the information about your event as interesting as you can, but always tell the truth.

You could also include a short letter, signed by all the club members, saying, "We would be very grateful if you would help us let the world know what we are doing." This might help convince the newsperson to use your release in the paper or on the air.

Stations and papers don't often get information of this kind from kids, so they might be very pleased to use your release. Rather than Special Delivery, why not send it First Class Male or Female, and deliver it in person, using one of your club members. If you do this, the chance of its being used would be even better. And although the biggest papers in your community will probably not print your release, a neighborhood paper certainly might.

Chapter 17
Giving a Helping Hand

Many clubs that last over a long period of time get their greatest pleasure from helping others. Your club can, too. There's so much you can do. You can share what you know, and you can share what you have. You'll be surprised how much of both you already have to give.

Here's a list that's bound to have a couple of items that are just right for your group.

1. Around the winter holidays collect baskets of good things for needy families. They could be filled with food, clothing, and toys donated by the families in your neighborhood. By acting as the collection point for people on your block, you'll be surprised at how much stuff you can gather. Put them into a big decorated paper grocery bag or carton, and ask the local police to deliver the holiday goods. They will deliver it to a family that really has a need, and it won't be embarrassing to the people, as it might be if your club members delivered the basket themselves.

2. Collect old toys before Christmas and bring them to police or fire stations. If the toy is not in tiptop condition, the police and firemen often have people who will paint and fix it up, then wrap and give it away. In this way, your club will have added a sparkle to some child's holiday whom Santa might otherwise have missed. You can also collect books and magazines for hospitals and old peoples' homes any time, and present them when you have a couple of boxes full.

3. Put on a play, puppet show, or magic performance for a local home for older people. Call up the director and find out if he will let your club put on the show for the people who live there. Generally, homes for older people do not get much entertainment. But residents love youngsters and

would be delighted to be entertained by you. You can also offer to perform at a children's nursery school or at an orphanage.

4. If you had a carnival and your booths and games were really good, put it on again—this time free of charge at your local orphanage. Your repeat performance will please them a lot.

5. Is there going to be a telethon on one of your local stations? Call the organization headquarters by checking the phone number for the Variety Club, United Cerebral Palsy, March of Dimes, or others in your city. Somone will tell you how you can help; maybe by collecting for them door-to-door (in pairs or groups, never alone), or as helpers at the auditorium of the TV station itself.

6. Local merchants, always eager to advertise and to look good in the community, will sponsor you if you want to raise money for a charity by either Pedaling for Profit or Walking for Wealth. Whether your Kids-Only Club wants to make the money to buy the materials for building birdfeeders, to give at a telethon, or to buy toys for an orphanage at Christmas, the technique is the same.

Ask a local storeowner (someone from whom you or your family regularly buy) if he or she will be your sponsor on the ride or walk. If it's a bike ride, keep it to three to five miles and ask the sponsor to pay you 50¢ or $1.00 a mile. If each member of your club gets a different sponsor, no one will be paying too much. What are they paying you for? For the paper sign on your back as you pedal (or walk) which says "(Name of sponsor) is paying me (amount) to raise money for (the purpose)." It's a kind of commercial that people are sure to notice, especially when all your club members wheel or march on by in style.

7. Keep your eyes peeled for other community activities and helping groups with whom your Kids-Only Club can participate in giving a helping hand. People are full of ideas all the time, and you should find plenty of things you can tackle all year long.

Chapter 18
Getting a Helping Hand

The Kids-Only Club is your club. It isn't guided by parents or other grownups, but there is nothing wrong now and then with getting a helping hand from adults. The help you get won't make your club any less of a Kids-Only Club, for you will still be in charge of the activities. What getting help from adults will do is to give you some suggestions, helpful information, a little assist on practical matters, and perhaps some extra money to get your club flying.

Here are some people who might benefit your club:

1. *Parents* might help by giving a little money to start your treasury and get the club rolling. They will probably be willing to do other things too, such as driving club members around, providing refreshments for meetings, offering advice (when you ask). But don't expect one parent to do it all. Get several volunteers. To find them, prepare the sample questionnaire at the end of this chapter and give to each club parent, as well as to other friendly adults in your neighborhood. With the answers, you'll get an idea of how much and what kind of help you can expect.

2. *Local adult service clubs,* like the Rotary Club, Kiwanis, Hadassah, and others, are often happy to help a newly organized group of kids with a small donation.

3. *Local storekeepers* sometimes want to encourage a well-organized youth club, especially if members buy what they sell. A sporting goods store might make a small donation to an athletic club (for special T-shirts), and a stamp store might be willing to help a stamp collecting club. Approaches by your president and treasurer could

bring excellent results. You will find that some adults would rather give money than time.

4. *Skilled men and women* in the neighborhood are often willing to come into a youth club meeting and give advice. One club of 11-year-old girls invited a local hairdresser to a meeting. He studied each girl's hairdo, suggested changes, gave suggestions on hair care, and even cut one girl's hair. The club learned a lot from this man, and he picked up several new customers.

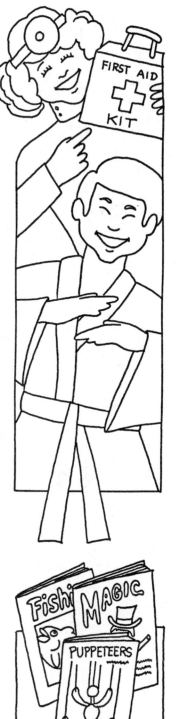

Doctors, paramedics, or nurses might come in and give a session on first aid. A hobbyist (like the coin dealer) might bring his own coin collection to a meeting just to share it with you, or he might arrange to take you to the home of a man who has the best collection in town. People who have collections of things they love *love* to show them off.

Almost every town in America has a martial arts school to teach judo and karate and other forms of unarmed self-defense. If you call the instructor, he might send his best students to put on a demonstration if he thinks there's a chance of picking up some new customers.

That kind of visit is good fun for your club and good business for the adults, too, who can introduce themselves and their service to club members and their families.

5. If you are a hobby club (all members are interested in one hobby: puppets, or magic, or tropical fish, or soapbox derby racers), see if your club can link up with a *national organization* that does what you like to do. For example, puppeteers can join the Puppeteers of America, magicians should contact the International Brotherhood of Magicians.

There is a special magazine for every hobby you can think of. You'll probably find copies in your local library or the librarian can track it down for your group. These magazines are pub-

lished by the important hobby guilds or organizations and in it will be mentioned the proper national group for you to contact.

Think about sending a questionnaire around your neighborhood to find adults who would be willing to help when you need help. What you want are people to give time, money, or skill—like driving you to the lumber shop or beach. Politicians use volunteer help for their activities, why shouldn't you?

The Sample Questionnaire for parents and friends could include these questions:

1. Would you be willing to help us pay for craft materials, tools, postage, etc.?

2. Would you share a certain amount of your time?

3. Would you be willing to take us places from time to time?

4. Would you be willing to cook or bake for a club activity?

5. Would you donate old clothes, shoes, toys, books, and other items to be used for costumes, garage and rummage sales, or as charity donations?

6. Do you have a place where our club can meet?

Be prepared to get some "Nos" and don't be hurt if people don't answer at all. The few "Yeses" you get will be gold mines for the club now—and in the future.

Now that you and your friends know how to set up and run a Kids-Only Club and how to go about organizing so many activities, you might also want to plan block parties, a pet-walking or baby-sitting service, a neighborhood talent show or swap meet; you might even try starting your own neighborhood newspaper. It's all up to you. You can do it.

Your club can be one of the nicest things you do with your friends.

Now go out and have a simply wonderful Kids-Only time.

Index